COOKING WITH

Bon Appétit

COOKING WITH
Bon Appétit

Poultry

THE KNAPP PRESS
Publishers
Los Angeles

Copyright © 1984 by Knapp Communications Corporation

Published by The Knapp Press
5900 Wilshire Boulevard, Los Angeles, California 90036

Library of Congress Cataloging in Publication Data

Main entry under title:

Poultry.

    (Cooking with Bon appétit)
    Includes index.
    1. Cookery (Poultry)   I. Bon appétit.   II. Series.
TX750.P6724   1984   641.6'65   83-24867
ISBN 0-89535-134-X

On the cover: *Chicken Legs with Basil Stuffing and Tomato-Zucchini Sauce*

Printed and bound in the United States of America
10 9 8 7 6 5 4 3 2

❧ Contents

Foreword . . . . *vii*

1 Chicken *1*

  Roasted and Baked 2
  Broiled 15
  Grilled 16
  Poached, Braised and Steamed 19
  Sautéed 29
  Stir-Fried 40
  Fried 43
  Salads and Sandwiches 47
  Livers 53

2 Turkey *55*

3 Duck and Goose *67*

  Duck 68
  Goose 80

4 Game Birds *83*

  Pheasant 84

Squab and Quail 85
Cornish Game Hens 89

5 Stuffings and Sauces 95
Stuffings 96
Sauces 107

Index .113

🍒 Foreword

Poultry—chicken, turkey, duck, goose and game birds—are among the most versatile ingredients available to the home cook. They take well to almost any preparation, from the simplest roasting with fresh herbs to more elaborate presentations such as pâtés and galantines. Piquantly spiced or delicately subtle, in salads or stews, sautéed, stuffed, broiled, poached or fried—and for lunch, brunch or dinner—poultry is reliably abundant, usually inexpensive and always thoroughly delicious.

Cooks all over the world agree: Poultry is a universal favorite. As this collection of recipes from the pages of *Bon Appétit* tantalizingly demonstrates, poultry is an international master of disguise. It can appear with the zip of Szechwan Spicy Tangerine Chicken (page 42) and Honey-brined Smoked Duck, (page 74) or with the refined elegance of Chicken Breasts with Pearl Onions and Gratin of Mixed Greens (page 9) or Pheasant Souvaroff (page 84).

Not to say that you won't find poultry here in intriguing variations of its more familiar guises. For instance, Braised Turkey with Lemon and Cinnamon (page 63) and Turkey Paupiettes with Creamed Chestnuts (page 61) are both dressed-up twists on a genuine American tradition. Braised Goose with Red Wine Sauce (page 82) and Smoked Herb-seasoned Quail (page 89) are classic specialties that are easy to prepare yet sophisticated enough for company. And to help turn even the simplest poultry dish into an occasion, there is also included a helpful chapter on stuffings and sauces—with enough variety from around the world to suit any menu.

Each chapter also contains tips and techniques to make preparation as easy as possible, including how to cut up and bone a whole chicken, simple steps to the perfect roast duck, and how to cook a turkey in a microwave oven.

Good cooks everywhere have put the advantages of poultry to delectable use throughout history. Now it is easy to follow in their footsteps and discover the wealth of culinary possibilities poultry can provide.

1 ❦ Chicken

Poets have always been unfair to chicken. There are lyrics to skylarks, odes to nightingales, sonnets for robins and epics on eagles. Swallows are celebrated in song and rhyme, and even the albatross has its ballad. But for the chicken, nary a limerick. Poets just take chicken for granted.

Not so cooks. In kitchens the world over, chicken is the most popular of all birds. This is not surprising when you consider that it is very economical, easy to prepare, highly nutritious, and tastes great in literally thousands of ways. In fact, nothing in the entire lexicon of gastronomy is more versatile than chicken: It can be roasted, baked, fried, steamed, sautéed, poached or grilled. It can be stuffed, sauced, breaded or basted, left whole, halved, boned or shredded. It marries well with myriad flavorings—from fruit to nuts, from the most delicate herb to the spiciest spice. And it is the easiest of all foods to plan a meal around—from a hearty, simple Sunday supper, to a casual luncheon salad or even a sophisticated and spectacular entrée worthy of the finest restaurant. Given all this, it is surely appropriate that our first and largest chapter is devoted entirely to chicken.

Virtually every national and ethnic cuisine boasts countless recipes for the bird. From India, for example, comes fragrant Chicken in Silky Almond Sauce (page 24), and from Thailand there are stuffed chicken wings served with a piquant chili-tamarind sauce (page 45). Germany offers a robust Chicken One-Pot with Dumplings (page 25), and from Russia comes an easy version of Chicken Kiev (page 11). From Hungary there is Creamy Paprika Chicken (page 24)—almost the national dish. In France, chicken becomes *poulet,* and it is offered *à la Bordelaise* (page 33) and *Dijonnaise* (page 16). And so on all around the globe, then back to the States, where chicken is butterflied and deviled (page 6), "beer-b-cued" (page 16) and, of course, Southern fried (page 43).

With this atlas of culinary riches, perhaps chicken doesn't need the poets after all. In the hands of a good cook, chicken is poetry itself.

🍎 Roasted and Baked

Roast Chicken with Rosemary Butter

A vertical roaster is good for this recipe as it cuts cooking time by at least 25 percent and requires little attention (all you have to do is adjust temperatures and set a timer).

2 servings

1 small garlic glove, minced
3 tablespoons unsalted butter, room temperature
Juice of 1 lemon
2 tablespoons fresh rosemary *or* 2 teaspoons dried
¼ teaspoon salt

⅛ teaspoon freshly ground pepper
1 2½- to 3-pound chicken, rinsed and patted dry
½ lemon
Sweet Hungarian paprika
½ cup water

If using vertical roaster, place rack in lowest position and preheat oven to 450°F. Combine garlic, butter, lemon juice, rosemary, salt and pepper in processor or blender and mix well (lemon may not blend in completely). Stuff mixture under skin of chicken in breast and thigh areas. Rub skin with cut lemon and sprinkle with paprika.

Set on vertical roaster (or on rack) in shallow roasting pan. Add water to pan and roast chicken 15 minutes. Reduce oven to 375°F and continue roasting until chicken is done (allow about 15 minutes to the pound if using vertical roaster or about 20 minutes to the pound if using regular rack). Cut into quarters using poultry shears.

English Roast Chicken with Herbed Orange Stuffing

6 servings

Herbed Orange Stuffing
1½ pounds ground veal
2 tablespoons (¼ stick) unsalted butter
1 large onion, minced
2 carrots, finely diced
4 cups fresh white breadcrumbs
¾ cup whipping cream (or slightly more)
½ cup minced fresh herbs (such as tarragon, parsley and thyme)
½ cup dried currants soaked in ⅓ cup fresh orange juice 30 minutes
½ cup chopped walnuts

1 teaspoon dried marjoram
1 teaspoon salt
Freshly ground pepper
Freshly grated nutmeg

1 5- to 6-pound chicken
¾ cup (1½ sticks) unsalted butter, room temperature
1 tablespoon minced fresh parsley
1 tablespoon honey
Grated peel of 1 lemon
Grated peel of 1 orange

Watercress sprigs (garnish)

For stuffing: Sauté veal in nonstick large skillet over medium-high heat until just beginning to lose pink color, about 3 minutes. Transfer to large bowl. Melt 2 tablespoons butter in same skillet over medium-high heat. Add onion and carrots and sauté until softened and just beginning to color. Blend into veal. Add breadcrumbs, ¾ cup cream, minced herbs, undrained currants, walnuts, marjoram, salt, pepper and nutmeg and toss gently (*mixture should just hold together*). Add small amount of cream if necessary.

Preheat oven to 375°F. Season main cavity of chicken with salt. Stuff main and neck cavities loosely. Truss chicken, then secure wings and legs with string.

Cream together butter, parsley, honey and citrus peels. Rub most of flavored butter over entire surface of chicken. Set chicken on rack in roasting pan. Tent with greased parchment paper. Roast 1 hour.

Baste chicken with pan juices and brush with remaining flavored butter. Continue roasting, basting frequently, until skin is rich golden brown and leg moves easily, about 1 hour.

Let stand 15 minutes on heated platter. Garnish platter with watercress. Nap chicken with pan juices and serve.

Sesame-crisped Chicken

4 servings

¼ cup soy sauce
2½ tablespoons dry Sherry
2 tablespoons vegetable oil
2 tablespoons orange marmalade
1 tablespoon honey
1 garlic clove, minced
1½ teaspoons sesame oil*

¼ teaspoon hot pepper sauce
4 chicken breast halves, skinned

6 3½-inch sesame breadsticks, crushed
2 tablespoons (¼ stick) butter

Combine first 8 ingredients in blender or processor and mix well. Pour into shallow baking dish. Add chicken and turn several times to coat evenly. Cover and chill several hours or overnight, turning occasionally.

Preheat oven to 375°F. Grease 9 × 9-inch baking dish. Drain chicken, reserving marinade. Arrange in single layer in prepared dish. Sprinkle with crushed breadsticks and dot with butter. Bake, basting frequently with reserved marinade, until chicken is tender and juices run clear when pricked with fork, about 25 minutes. Serve hot.

*Available in oriental markets.

Yogurt Chicken

8 servings

4 to 5 pounds chicken pieces, skinned
2 to 3 garlic cloves, minced
½ teaspoon fines herbes
¼ teaspoon freshly ground pepper
3 cups plain yogurt
2 onions, finely chopped

3 tablespoons fresh lemon juice
1½ teaspoons soy sauce
1½ teaspoons turmeric
¾ teaspoon ground ginger
½ teaspoon cinnamon
½ teaspoon ground cloves

Rub chicken with garlic, fines herbes and pepper. Combine remaining ingredients in large bowl. Add chicken, turning to coat well. Cover and marinate in refrigerator 24 hours, turning occasionally.

Preheat oven to 350°F. Remove chicken from marinade and place in single layer in large roasting pan. Tent with foil and bake 30 minutes. Remove foil, turn pieces and bake about 30 minutes longer or until lightly browned, basting occasionally with marinade. Serve immediately.

❦ The Vertically Roasted Chicken

The vertical roaster (made by several manufacturers) helps chicken cook to tender, crisp perfection virtually fat free. Season the bird with wine, tuck a variety of seasonings under the skin, or add liquid flavorings with a culinary injector. Here are some simple and flavorful recipes.

Basic Vertically Roasted Chicken

1 3- to 3½-pound chicken	1 tablespoon dry white wine
½ cup water	½ teaspoon paprika

Place rack in lowest position of oven and preheat to 450°F. Rinse chicken under cold water and pat dry thoroughly with paper towels. Gently press chicken onto vertical roaster. Set roaster in 8- or 9-inch cake pan. Add ½ cup water. Roast 15 minutes. Reduce heat to 375°F; continue roasting an additional 15 minutes per pound. During last 20 minutes of cooking, combine wine and paprika in small bowl and blend well. Brush over chicken several times to aid browning.

Oriental Chicken

4 servings

1 large garlic clove, minced	1 tablespoon firmly packed
3 tablespoons soy sauce	brown sugar
2 tablespoons cider vinegar	1 3- to 3½-pound chicken

Combine garlic, soy sauce, vinegar and brown sugar in bowl, blending well.

Loosen skin from chicken breast, thighs and drumsticks with fingers *(be careful not to puncture skin)*. Rub or spoon sauce under skin. Roast as directed in basic instructions, basting with sauce and pan juices.

Chicken with Garlic and Basil Puree

4 servings

3 garlic cloves, unpeeled	1 3- to 3½-pound chicken
3 tablespoons fresh basil *or* 1	
tablespoon dried	
Pinch of salt	

Bring 1½ cups water to boil in medium saucepan over medium-high heat. Add garlic and cook 30 minutes. Drain well.

Peel garlic. Transfer to processor or blender. Add basil and salt and puree until smooth. Loosen skin from chicken breast, thighs and drumsticks with fingers *(be careful not to puncture skin)*. Rub or spoon sauce under skin. Roast as directed in basic instructions, basting with wine-paprika mixture.

Lime and Green Chili Chicken

4 servings

2 fresh *or* canned mild green chilies, minced
1 green onion, minced
¼ cup fresh lime juice
Minced fresh cilantro (coriander)
1 3- to 3½-pound chicken

Combine chilies, green onion, lime juice and cilantro in small bowl.

Loosen skin from chicken breast, thighs and drumsticks with fingers *(be careful not to puncture skin)*. Rub or spoon sauce under skin. Roast as directed in basic instructions, omitting wine-paprika mixture.

Cognac and Port Chicken

4 servings

3 tablespoons Cognac
3 tablespoons Port
½ teaspoon onion juice
1 3- to 3½-pound chicken
¼ teaspoon dried thyme

Combine Cognac, Port and onion juice in small bowl. Pour mixture into culinary injector and press into chicken breasts, thighs and legs. Sprinkle chicken with thyme. Roast as directed in basic instructions, basting with wine-paprika mixture.

Chicken with Sweet Spices

4 servings

1 large garlic clove, minced
3 tablespoons fresh lemon juice
1 tablespoon soy sauce
1 teaspoon honey
⅛ teaspoon ground ginger
⅛ teaspoon cardamom
⅛ teaspoon allspice
Generous pinch of ground cumin
1 3- to 3½-pound chicken

Combine garlic, lemon juice, soy sauce, honey, ginger, cardamom, allspice and cumin in small bowl.

Loosen skin from chicken breast, thighs and drumsticks with fingers *(be careful not to puncture skin)*. Rub or spoon sauce under skin. Roast as directed in basic instructions, omitting wine-paprika mixture.

Mustard Chicken

3 to 4 servings

¼ cup Dijon mustard
3 garlic cloves, finely minced
1 3- to 4-pound chicken, cut into serving pieces

2 teaspoons dried rosemary
Freshly ground pepper
½ cup freshly grated Parmesan cheese

Preheat oven to 350°F. Combine mustard and garlic in small bowl. Arrange chicken in single layer in baking dish. Brush mustard mixture generously over each piece. Sprinkle with rosemary and pepper. Top with Parmesan. Bake until juices run clear when pricked with a fork, about 45 to 55 minutes. Serve hot or cold.

Butterflied Deviled Chicken

6 servings

½ cup prepared hot mustard (preferably English, German *or* Chinese)
1 large shallot
3 tablespoons cider vinegar
2 teaspoons honey
Generous pinch of freshly ground pepper

2 3-pound chickens, butterflied*

¼ cup (½ stick) butter, melted
Parsley sprigs (garnish)

Combine mustard, shallot, vinegar, honey and pepper in processor or blender and mix until smooth. Reserve ¼ cup of mixture for basting and refrigerate. Transfer remaining mixture to small bowl. Loosen skin from flesh of chicken breast, thighs and legs with fingers *(be careful not to puncture skin)*. Using fingers, spread mustard mixture smoothly between meat and skin. Pull any extra skin over breast and fasten with small skewer. Refrigerate until ready to roast.

Arrange chicken skin side up on rack in shallow roasting pan. Brush with melted butter and reserved mustard mixture. Transfer to 375°F oven. Roast about 20 minutes. Turn chicken over; repeat basting. Roast another 20 to 25 minutes. Turn chicken again and continue roasting, basting as necessary, until tender, about 15 to 20 minutes. To serve, cut chicken into quarters and arrange on heated platter. Garnish with parsley sprigs.

*To butterfly chicken, cut down middle of backbone, then loosen meat by scraping down each side of backbone with boning knife, keeping knife against bone. Turn chicken over, skin side up, and flatten by pounding with palm of hand. Turn again and slip out breastbones with sharp small knife, being careful to keep skin intact.

Oven-fried Buttermilk Chicken

4 servings

½ cup freshly grated Parmesan cheese
½ cup wheat germ
½ teaspoon dried rosemary
½ teaspoon onion powder
½ teaspoon salt

¼ teaspoon dried thyme
¼ teaspoon garlic powder
⅛ teaspoon freshly ground pepper
8 chicken thighs
¾ cup buttermilk

Preheat oven to 325°F. Lightly grease baking sheet. Combine all ingredients except chicken and buttermilk in pie plate or shallow dish. Dip chicken in buttermilk, then roll in dry mixture and place on baking sheet. Bake until juices run clear when chicken is pricked with a fork, about 50 minutes.

Chicken Breasts with Chinese Mushrooms
(Blanc de Poulet au Champignons Chinoises)

Serve as an entrée, with rice and broccoli on a side plate. Do not add salt to the ginger-scented sauce, as these mushrooms have a high sodium content.

4 servings

4 large chicken breast halves, boned, skinned, and tendons removed
Butter, melted
Coarse salt
Freshly ground white pepper

Sauce
8 medium-size oriental dried mushrooms
¾ cup warm water
1½ cups chicken stock

½ cup dry white wine
1 tablespoon minced shallot
1 teaspoon minced fresh ginger
½ teaspoon minced garlic

¾ cup whipping cream
2½ tablespoons glace de viande (meat glaze)*
⅓ cup drained canned Chinese straw mushrooms

¼ cup chopped fresh chives

Press each chicken breast down and butterfly by slicing in half horizontally using a long thin knife placed parallel to the board, stopping just before you cut all the way through. Open up as you would a book. With your fingers, press to flatten into a neat, thin piece.

Lightly brush 4 ovenproof plates with melted butter and sprinkle lightly with salt and pepper. Place chicken breasts in center of each plate. Brush lightly with butter and sprinkle with pepper. Press small piece of waxed paper on top of each breast. Set aside while preparing sauce.

For sauce: Soak mushrooms in warm water 15 minutes. Drain well (reserve soaking liquid); squeeze out excess moisture. Remove stems and slice into strips; set caps and stems aside.

Pour soaking liquid into medium saucepan. Add stock, wine, shallot, ginger and garlic and cook over medium heat until reduced to about 1 cup. *(Can be prepared several hours ahead to this point.)*

Stir in cream and glace de viande and continue cooking until sauce is slightly reduced, about 5 to 8 minutes. Add rehydrated and straw mushrooms and continue cooking until about 1 cup of sauce remains. Preheat oven to 450°F.

Blend chives into sauce. Season to taste with white pepper. Keep warm.

Bake chicken 5 minutes. Remove plates from oven and discard waxed paper. Divide sauce evenly and spoon over chicken. Serve immediately.

*Available at specialty food stores.

Chicken in Apple Brandy Sauce

6 servings

6 large chicken breast halves, boned and skinned
All purpose flour
Salt and freshly ground pepper

¼ cup duck fat *or* 2 tablespoons (¼ stick) butter plus 2 tablespoons oil

3 pippin apples, peeled, cored and thickly sliced
½ cup dry white wine
¾ cup sparkling apple cider

¾ cup Calvados
1½ cups chicken stock (preferably homemade)
½ cup chicken Demi-glace (see recipe, page 109)
1 cup whipping cream
¼ cup (½ stick) chilled unsalted butter, cut into small pieces
½ teaspoon freshly ground white pepper or to taste
Fresh lemon juice (optional)

Sprinkle chicken with flour, shaking off excess. Season with salt and pepper.

Preheat oven to 400°F. Melt duck fat in heavy large skillet over high heat. Add chicken and brown on both sides. Transfer to baking pan (do not clean skillet) and place in oven until cooked through. Remove chicken from oven and keep warm.

Add apples to same skillet, place over medium-high heat and toss briefly to coat with pan juices. Pour off excess fat. Add wine to skillet and bring to boil, scraping up brown bits. Add cider and boil until reduced by half, about 6 to 7 minutes. Add Calvados and ignite, shaking skillet gently until flame subsides. Stir in stock and Demi-glace and boil until reduced by half, about 8 to 10 minutes. Add cream and boil until sauce is thick enough to coat back of spoon, about 15 minutes. Whisk in butter. Taste and adjust seasoning with salt and white pepper, adding small amount of fresh lemon juice if sauce seems too sweet.

Divide chicken breasts among heated plates. Fan apple slices atop chicken. Spoon sauce over and serve immediately.

Chicken with Asparagus and Lemon Sabayon

2 to 4 servings

1½ pounds asparagus, trimmed and peeled
Salt and freshly ground pepper

1 large lemon (garnish)

4 large chicken breast halves, boned, skinned, and tendons removed

¼ cup (½ stick) unsalted butter
Fresh lemon juice

Lemon Sabayon
6 egg yolks

½ cup chicken stock (preferably homemade)
½ cup whipping cream
2 tablespoons Armagnac *or* brandy
1½ to 2 tablespoons fresh lemon juice
1½ teaspoons minced fresh thyme, tarragon *or* marjoram, *or* ½ teaspoon dried

1 tablespoon minced fresh chives (garnish)

Bring large stockpot of salted water to boil over medium-high heat. Add asparagus and cook until tender when pierced with knife, about 5 to 8 minutes. Remove with tongs (reserving cooking liquid) and plunge into ice water to stop cooking process; drain well and pat dry. Cut tip ends of spears into 5-inch lengths (use asparagus stems in soups or salads). Sprinkle with salt and pepper. Set aside.

Using zester, remove 6 equally spaced strips of peel from stem to tip of lemon. Cut lemon into thin rounds; discard seeds. Boil 10 minutes in reserved liquid. Drain well and set aside.

Preheat oven to 425°F. Gently pound chicken breasts between sheets of waxed paper until evenly flattened.

Melt butter in large gratin or other shallow baking pan over medium heat. Remove from heat and add chicken, turning to coat well. Sprinkle with lemon juice, salt and pepper. Cover chicken with buttered parchment paper. Cover pan and bake until chicken is opaque and springy to the touch, about 6 minutes. Drain; keep warm.

For sabayon: Combine yolks, stock, cream, Armagnac, lemon juice, thyme, and salt and pepper in top of double boiler set over simmering water. Whisk until mixture thickens and doubles in volume, about 3 minutes.

Preheat broiler. Transfer chicken to heatproof serving platter, surround with asparagus and garnish with lemon slices. Spoon sabayon over top and sprinkle with chives. Run under broiler until sauce is brown and bubbly, about 3 minutes. Serve immediately.

Chicken Breasts with Pearl Onions and Gratin of Mixed Greens

Spinach, watercress, arugula, escarole or fennel can also be used in gratin.

4 to 6 servings

1 pound small button mushrooms
¾ cup chicken stock (preferably homemade)
1 tablespoon fresh lemon juice
1½ teaspoons minced fresh thyme *or* ½ teaspoon dried

24 to 26 pearl onions*

2 tablespoons (¼ stick) unsalted butter
½ cup chicken stock (preferably homemade)
¾ teaspoon minced fresh thyme *or* ¼ teaspoon dried

Gratin of Mixed Greens
1½ cups fine julienne of Belgian endive
1½ cups fine julienne of cored savoy *or* green cabbage
1½ cups fine julienne of romaine
2 tablespoons (¼ stick) unsalted butter
⅓ cup chicken stock (preferably homemade)
⅔ cup sorrel (6 ounces), stemmed and cut into fine julienne slices
1 tablespoon fresh lemon juice

2¼ teaspoons minced fresh thyme *or* ¾ teaspoon dried
⅛ teaspoon freshly grated nutmeg
Salt and freshly ground pepper
1 cup whipping cream (or more)

Chicken
4 large chicken breast halves, boned, skinned, and tendons removed
¼ cup (½ stick) unsalted butter
Fresh lemon juice
Salt and freshly ground pepper

Sauce
½ cup dry white wine *or* dry vermouth
½ cup whipping cream
1 teaspoon fresh lemon juice
¾ teaspoon minced fresh thyme *or* ¼ teaspoon dried
⅛ teaspoon freshly grated nutmeg
1 tablespoon brandy *or* Armagnac
Salt and freshly ground pepper
2 tablespoons (¼ stick) unsalted butter

Freshly cooked rice

Combine mushrooms, ¾ cup stock, lemon juice and thyme in medium saucepan. Cover, place over medium-high heat and bring to boil. Reduce heat and simmer 3 minutes, stirring occasionally. Remove from heat. Let mushrooms cool in cooking liquid, stirring occasionally. Drain mushrooms well, reserving cooking liquid.

Cut an *X* in root end of onions to prevent bursting while cooking. Blanch onions in large saucepan of boiling water, about 1 minute. Drain and peel.

Melt 2 tablespoons butter in heavy large skillet over medium-high heat. Stir in onions. Add ½ cup stock with thyme. Reduce heat to low, cover and cook, stirring occasionally, until onions are tender when pierced with knife, about 30 minutes. Drain well and add cooking liquid to reserved mushroom liquid. Add onions to mushrooms.

For gratin: Preheat oven to 425°F. Wash endive, cabbage and romaine but do not dry. Melt 2 tablespoons butter in large heavy skillet or ovenproof baking dish over medium-high heat. Gradually stir in greens. Add ⅓ cup stock, cover and cook, stirring occasionally, about 5 minutes. Increase heat to high, add sorrel and cook until wilted. Stir in lemon juice, thyme, nutmeg and salt and pepper. Remove from heat. Mix in 1 cup cream, blending well. Bake, stirring occasionally, until cream is absorbed, about 15 minutes. (If mixture becomes dry while baking, stir in additional cream.) Taste and adjust seasoning. Set aside.

For chicken: Gently pound chicken breasts between sheets of waxed paper until evenly flattened. Melt ¼ cup butter in large gratin or other shallow baking pan over medium heat. Remove from heat and add chicken, turning to coat well. Sprinkle with lemon juice and salt and pepper. Cover chicken with buttered parchment or waxed paper. Cover pan and bake until chicken is opaque and springy to the touch, about 6 minutes. Drain; keep warm.

For sauce: Add wine to reserved onion and mushroom cooking liquids. Place over high heat and boil until reduced to ¾ cup. Stir in remaining cream, lemon juice, thyme and nutmeg. Boil until thickened and reduced to ¾ cup. Add brandy and salt and pepper. Whisk in 2 tablespoons butter. Keep warm.

Just before serving, reheat mushrooms and onions briefly in medium saucepan over medium-high heat. Sprinkle with salt and pepper. (If necessary, reheat vegetable gratin in same manner.) Divide gratin evenly and center on heated plates. Arrange chicken breasts diagonally over gratin. Surround with mushrooms and onions. Tightly pack rice into ½-cup molds or ice cream scoop and unmold onto plates. Spoon sauce over chicken and rice and serve.

*Sixteen to 20 small white boiling onions can be substituted for pearl onions. Increase cooking time to 50 minutes.

Papillotes of Chicken with Almond-Mustard Sauce

Plump, tender chicken breasts baked on a bed of crisp, savory vegetables, with each portion wrapped in its own parchment envelope—perhaps the essence of one-dish dining. Let guests open their own packets. Serve with a California Petite Sirah or Zinfandel. Recipe can be doubled easily.

6 servings

3 tablespoons clarified unsalted butter*
18 green onions, white part only, quartered lengthwise
9 small carrots, peeled and cut into 3/16 × ¼ × 2-inch sticks (french-fry cutter works well)
6 medium turnips, peeled and cut into 3/16 × ¼ × 2-inch sticks (french-fry cutter works well)
Salt and freshly ground pepper
6 tablespoons dry vermouth
3 ounces (about ⅔ cup) slivered almonds, lightly toasted

3 tablespoons clarified unsalted butter

8 medium shallots, minced, *or* 8 green onions and 1 small garlic clove, minced
6 tablespoons dry vermouth
2 cups unsalted chicken stock (preferably homemade)
3 ounces (about ⅔ cup) slivered almonds, lightly toasted and ground
¼ cup whipping cream
2 tablespoons Dijon mustard *or* German mustard
6 drops almond extract

6 chicken breast halves, boned, skinned and sliced diagonally into 5 pieces
Oil

Heat 3 tablespoons clarified butter in heavy nonaluminum large skillet over high heat. Add onions, carrots and turnips and stir-fry until lightly browned, 2 to 3 minutes. Season lightly with salt and pepper. Blend in 6 tablespoons vermouth and boil until evaporated. Remove from heat. Sprinkle with slivered almonds. Remove vegetable mixture from skillet using slotted spoon and set aside.

Heat remaining 3 tablespoons clarified butter in same skillet over medium-high heat. Add shallots and sauté until golden. Add 6 tablespoons vermouth and stir, scraping up any browned bits. Cook until reduced to thin glaze (about 2 tablespoons). Blend in stock and reduce to ½ cup. Stir in ground almonds, cream and mustard and boil about 30 seconds. Remove from heat. Blend in almond extract. Taste and adjust seasoning. Set sauce aside to cool.

Cut six 12 × 24-inch pieces of parchment paper or aluminum foil. Fold each piece in half lengthwise, then cut each folded piece into half of heart shape to form heart when unfolded (cut to edges to make as large a heart as possible). Unfold 1 heart in front of you. Spoon about ⅙ of vegetable mixture in mound in center of 1 side. Top with 5 pieces of chicken (half breast). Spoon some of cooled sauce over chicken. Lightly brush opposite side of parchment with oil to prevent sticking. Fold opposite side of paper over chicken mixture, then roll and tuck edges to seal, leaving as much space inside as possible to allow for expansion from steam during cooking. Repeat with remaining vegetable mixture. *(Papillotes can be prepared 24 hours ahead to this point and refrigerated. Bring to room temperature before baking.)*

Arrange 1 rack in upper third of oven and another rack in lower third and preheat to 475°F. Arrange papillotes evenly on 2 large baking sheets. Bake exactly 20 minutes. Immediately transfer to heated dinner plates and serve.

*For clarified butter, melt ½ cup (1 stick) butter in medium saucepan over medium heat. Skim foam from top. Strain off clear liquid, discarding milky residue in bottom of pan. Store in refrigerator in tightly covered container. (Makes about 6 tablespoons.)

Oven-baked Chicken Kiev

4 servings

4 chicken breast halves, boned
¼ cup (½ stick) butter, room temperature
½ teaspoon dried tarragon

½ cup all purpose flour
2 eggs, beaten
1 cup dry breadcrumbs
Butter, melted (optional)

Preheat oven to 425°F. Lightly butter 8-inch square baking dish. Pound chicken to ¼-inch thickness. Combine ¼ cup butter and tarragon in small bowl and blend well. Place equal portions of butter mixture in center of chicken breasts. Fold ends over and tuck in sides, securing with toothpicks if necessary. Roll chicken in flour. Dip in eggs, then coat with breadcrumbs, covering completely. Arrange in prepared baking dish. Bake until golden brown, about 20 to 25 minutes, basting several times with melted butter if desired. Serve immediately.

🍎 Cutting and Boning Chicken

Food trends come and go, but no matter what the latest fancy, no one ever seems to tire of chicken. And a cut-up bird is probably the essence of versatility: A whole chicken can be presented only roasted, poached or braised, but once it is cut up, the possibilities are practically unlimited.

Dividing a whole chicken into easier-to-handle pieces is an appealing way for singles, couples and small families to have good, nutritious entrées on hand. Doing the cutting yourself ensures freshness, but best of all is price—check the difference in cost per pound between whole and cut-up poultry the next time you are at the market.

In addition to the methods of preparation already mentioned, the individual parts can be broiled, fried or sautéed. Breasts, legs and thighs can be served plain, sauced or with stuffing under the skin. After the bones have been removed, the meat can be pounded thin and fixed like scaloppine, or rolled around a savory filling. Wings can be simmered Chinese style or formed into miniature drumsticks for appetizers. Even the back can be added to the pot for a rich homemade stock.

All that's required is a sharp knife and sensitive fingertips to pinpoint the place to cut. When you are finished, there will be 12 pieces, along with fat that can be rendered and used in cooking, and trimmings and giblets for the stockpot. If breasts or legs are boned out, their scraps can be added to stock as well. The liver, which is too highly flavored for stock, can be served either with the chicken or sautéed for an omelet.

Cutting

1. Chill the chicken for ease in cutting.

2. Remove giblets from cavity; pull out fat from neck and tail.

3. Bend one wing tip backward to crack second wing joint, then cut through joint. Repeat with second wing tip. (Reserve wing tips for homemade stock.)

4. Pull one wing out from body to see where it attaches to shoulder. Locate ball and socket joint with finger, then cut through joint to remove wing. Repeat with second wing.

5. Place chicken on back. Pull one leg (drumstick and thigh) out from body. With knife slanted toward body, cut down through skin between back of thigh and body to reach hip joint. Bend thigh backward until hip joint pops out. Cut through hip joint to free thigh. Remove second leg in the same manner.

6. (If legs are to be boned for stuffing, omit this step and see directions for boning.) With finger, feel where drumstick and thigh are joined. Cut through joint to separate. Repeat with other leg.

7. Resting chicken on its shoulder with tail up, support back with one hand while cutting front from back at juncture between front and back ribs. Bend backbone away from collarbone and cut through exposed joint to sever connection between breast and back.

8. Bend back in half where rib cage ends and cut through this point to divide back into 2 pieces.

9. (If breast is to be boned, omit this step and see directions for boning.) Place breast, skin side down, with pointed narrow tip at the top. Make a slit down center of opaque white cartilage, continuing through thin membrane that covers broad keel bone (breastbone). Bend tip of breast backward where cartilage meets breastbone until breastbone pops out. Pull out breastbone while freeing meat from each side of it with fingers. Fold breast in half lengthwise, skin side in, pushing down hard at neck to break wishbone. Cut breast in half lengthwise.

Boning Legs
The drumstick should be connected to the thighbone for this procedure.

1. Place leg skin side down. Make a slit along the side of the thighbone, continuing it down center of drumstick.

2. Hold hip end of thigh with one hand. Gradually release thigh by scraping meat off bone on all sides. Remove thigh by cutting through socket where it articulates with drumstick, being careful not to pierce through the skin.

3. Cut around head of drumstick to free it, then bone out completely, following instructions for thigh.

4. Cut out cartilage from kneecap, again being careful not to pierce skin. Remove each tendon by holding onto end and scraping off meat as you pull it out.

5. To prepare meat, gently pound legs between two pieces of plastic wrap so that legs are of uniform thickness. Place meat side up. Sprinkle with salt and pepper. Fill lightly with favorite stuffing, leaving ¼-inch border on all sides. Fold in half and sew edges together with butcher's twine. Steam, sauté or bake until juices run clear and meat starts to feel springy, about 35 to 40 minutes. Discard string before serving.

Chicken Legs with Basil Stuffing and Tomato-Zucchini Sauce

Serve this savory mélange hot or cold.

2 to 4 servings

Tomato Zucchini Sauce
¼ pound zucchini (about 1 small)
   Pinch of salt

2 tablespoons (¼ stick) unsalted butter
¼ cup minced fresh basil
1 small garlic clove, minced
1½ tablespoons minced shallot
   Juice of 1 large lemon
⅓ cup olive oil
2 large tomatoes, peeled, seeded, juiced and coarsely chopped
   Salt and freshly ground pepper

Basil Stuffing*
3 tablespoons olive oil
1½ tablespoons minced shallot
3 tablespoons fine breadcrumbs
½ cup ricotta cheese (preferably whole milk)

½ cup grated imported Bel Paese cheese (about 2 ounces)
¼ cup plus 2 tablespoons freshly grated Parmesan cheese
1 egg yolk
1 small garlic clove, minced
2½ tablespoons minced fresh basil
1½ tablespoons unsalted butter, room temperature
   Salt and freshly ground pepper

Chicken
4 large chicken legs with thighs attached, skin left on

4 basil sprigs (garnish)

For sauce: Grate zucchini over colander; sprinkle lightly with salt. Let drain 30 minutes. Rinse; squeeze dry.

Melt butter in heavy small skillet over medium-high heat. Add zucchini and stir until cooked, about 3 minutes. Transfer to bowl. Stir in basil, garlic, shallot and lemon juice. Whisk in olive oil 1 drop at a time. Mix in tomatoes and salt and pepper to taste. Set aside.

For stuffing: Heat olive oil in small skillet over medium heat. Add shallot and stir until translucent, about 3 minutes. Mix in breadcrumbs, coating well. Remove from heat and let cool to room temperature. Using fork, mix in ricotta, Bel Paese, Parmesan, egg yolk, garlic, basil, butter and salt and pepper.

For chicken: Preheat oven to 325°F. Generously butter large gratin or other shallow baking pan and set aside.

Pat chicken legs dry. Gently loosen skin from legs with fingers (being careful not to pierce skin) as far down legs as possible. Spread layer of stuffing under loosened skin. Transfer chicken to prepared pan. Bake, basting occasionally until juices run clear when pierced with fork, about 40 to 45 minutes. Transfer to serving platter and tent with foil to keep warm.

Discard all fat from pan. Add sauce, place over medium-high heat and bring to boil. Let boil 2 minutes, scraping up any browned bits clinging to bottom of pan. Pour sauce over chicken. Arrange white paper frills on legs if desired. Garnish chicken with basil and serve.

*Basil Stuffing can also be used with roast chicken. Sauté minced liver with shallot. After adding basil, stir in 1 small tomato, peeled, seeded, juiced and chopped.

🍎 Broiled

Broiled Ginger Chicken

4 servings

4 8-ounce chicken legs with thighs attached
4 small garlic cloves
1 4-ounce piece fresh ginger, cut into ¼-inch slices
Grated peel of 1 large lemon
½ teaspoon salt
½ teaspoon freshly ground pepper
½ cup fresh cilantro (coriander) leaves

¼ cup fresh lemon juice
2 tablespoons Sherry vinegar
4 teaspoons peanut oil

Cilantro (coriander) sprigs (garnish)
8 lime wedges (garnish)

Using very sharp knife, score chicken skin diagonally, spacing cuts about ¼ inch apart. Arrange chicken in single layer in baking dish skin side up. With machine running, drop garlic and ginger through feed tube of processor and mince finely. Mix in lemon peel and salt and pepper. Add cilantro and mince finely. Blend in lemon juice and vinegar. With machine running, add oil through feed tube in thin stream. Rub mixture over both sides of chicken. Set aside for 2 to 3 hours.

Grease broiler pan and position about 4 inches from heat source. Preheat broiler. Transfer chicken to heated pan. Broil chicken until just tender, very juicy and deep golden, about 10 to 15 minutes on each side, turning chicken skin side up during last 2 to 3 minutes and brushing with any remaining ginger mixture. Transfer chicken to platter. Let stand 5 minutes. Garnish with cilantro and lime.

Chicken with Peanut Dipping Sauce

Serve hot or chilled. Cooked shrimp can be substituted for chicken.

4 to 6 servings

¼ cup light vegetable oil (preferably cold-pressed safflower)
1 teaspoon fresh lemon juice
½ teaspoon finely chopped garlic
½ teaspoon ground cumin
¼ teaspoon herb salt *or* vegetable salt
4 to 8 chicken breast halves, skinned and boned

Peanut Dipping Sauce
⅔ cup half and half *or* double-strength reconstituted nonfat dry milk

6 tablespoons peanut butter
3 tablespoons tamari soy sauce
1 tablespoon light vegetable oil (preferably cold-pressed safflower)
1 tablespoon fresh lemon juice
1 teaspoon finely chopped garlic
1 teaspoon dry mustard

Preheat broiler. Combine oil, lemon juice, garlic, cumin and herb salt in small bowl. Arrange chicken in broiler pan and brush with oil mixture. Broil chicken, turning once or twice, until cooked through, about 10 minutes.

For sauce: Combine all ingredients in small saucepan and blend with whisk. Bring to boil over medium heat, stirring constantly. Reduce heat and simmer 3 minutes, stirring occasionally. Serve with broiled chicken.

Chicken Teriyaki

3 to 4 servings

½ cup soy sauce
¼ cup fresh orange juice *or* apple juice
2 tablespoons vegetable oil
2 tablespoons vinegar
2 tablespoons saké *or* light dry Sherry

1 tablespoon honey
Finely grated orange peel to taste
2 teaspoons grated fresh ginger *or* 1 teaspoon ground ginger
1 2½- to 3-pound chicken, cut into 8 pieces

Combine first 8 ingredients in blender and mix well. Pour into deep bowl and add chicken. Cover and marinate in refrigerator up to 4 days, turning occasionally.

When ready to cook, preheat broiler. Arrange chicken pieces in shallow pan. Broil about 6 inches from heat until done, 15 to 20 minutes, turning frequently and basting with marinade. Heat remaining marinade and serve as sauce.

🍒 *Grilled*

Beer-b-cued Chicken

A family picnic favorite served either hot or cold.

4 servings

1 cup (2 sticks) butter
1 3-pound chicken, cut up

1 14-ounce bottle barbecue sauce
1 cup beer

Preheat oven to 350°F. Melt ½ cup butter in 9 × 13-inch pan. Add chicken; turn to coat. Bake 30 minutes.

Meanwhile, melt remaining butter with barbecue sauce and beer in medium saucepan over medium-high heat. Bring to boil, stirring constantly. Remove from heat and set aside.

Preheat broiler or prepare barbecue grill. Dip chicken in sauce. Arrange skin side down on rack over broiler pan or on grill. Cook, turning and basting frequently with sauce until browned and juices run clear when chicken is pricked with a fork, about 10 to 20 minutes for broiler or about 30 minutes for barbecue. Dip chicken in sauce again. Transfer to platter and serve. Pass any remaining sauce separately at table.

Grilled Chicken Dijonnais

6 servings

½ cup oil
¼ cup fresh lemon juice
½ teaspoon freshly ground pepper
6 8-ounce chicken breast halves, skinned and boned

3 tablespoons tarragon vinegar
2 tablespoons dry white wine

1 teaspoon dried tarragon
½ teaspoon freshly ground white pepper
16 tablespoons (2 sticks) butter
2 tablespoons strong Dijon mustard

Lemon slices (garnish)
Parsley sprigs (garnish)

Combine oil, lemon juice and pepper in shallow dish. Swirl chicken in mixture to coat. Cover with plastic wrap and marinate in refrigerator 30 minutes.

Meanwhile, combine vinegar and wine in heavy small saucepan and boil over medium-high heat until liquid is reduced to about 2 tablespoons. Remove from heat and add tarragon and pepper. Whisk in butter 1 tablespoon at a time, blending thoroughly after each addition. Place over low heat and continue whisking until sauce has thickened slightly. Whisk in mustard. Set aside and keep warm.

Prepare charcoal grill. Drain chicken well. Grill 3 to 4 minutes on each side. Arrange on heated platter. Garnish with lemon slices and parsley. Serve warm sauce separately.

Singapore Saté

Serve with onion slices and cucumber.

4 servings

4 small red onions, chopped
2 garlic cloves, chopped
4 teaspoons ground lemongrass
1 teaspoon ground coriander
1 teaspoon ground cumin
1 teaspoon ground ginger
Salt
Sugar
1 pound boneless white *or* dark chicken meat, cut into 1-inch cubes

¼ cup vegetable oil

Sauce
4 small red onions, chopped
8 dried small red chilies, soaked in water until soft
2 garlic cloves
4 candle nuts* *or* macadamia nuts
¼ cup peanut oil
6 ounces ground peanuts (about 1 cup shelled peanuts)
¼ cup tamarind water* *or* fresh lemon juice
¾ cup water
Salt
Sugar

Combine onions, garlic, lemongrass, coriander, cumin and ginger in processor or blender and mix until smooth. Stir in salt and sugar to taste. Transfer to large bowl. Add chicken and toss lightly. Marinate chicken mixture 1 hour.

Prepare barbecue grill. Thread chicken evenly onto skewers. Grill until just tender, turning and basting with oil.

Meanwhile, for sauce: Combine onions, small chilies, garlic and nuts in processor or blender and mix until smooth. Heat peanut oil in wok or small saucepan. Add onion mixture and fry 5 minutes. Stir in ground peanuts and tamarind water. Add water, salt and sugar to taste and bring to boil. Reduce heat and simmer until mixture thickens.

Arrange satés on platter and serve immediately. Pass sauce separately.

* Available in oriental markets.

Japanese Chicken Yakitori

6 main-course servings

Marinade
½ cup Japanese soy sauce
¼ cup saké *or* dry Sherry
¼ cup water
½ to 1 tablespoon brown sugar
1 to 1½ teaspoons grated fresh ginger

3 pounds chicken breasts, boned, skinned and cut into 1½-inch cubes

6 green onions, white part only, cut into 1-inch lengths

Chopped chives (garnish)
Green onion (garnish)

For marinade: Combine all ingredients in saucepan. Simmer 1 minute; cool. Alternately thread chicken and green onions onto wooden skewers.
   Prepare hibachi or barbecue, or preheat broiler. Dip skewers into marinade, coating well. Cook 3 to 4 inches from heat, basting frequently or dipping skewers back into marinade, until crisp and well glazed, about 4 to 5 minutes on each side. Sprinkle with chives and green onion and serve hot.

Italian Grilled Chicken on Skewers

If preparing skewers ahead and planning to reheat, slightly undercook chicken.

12 servings

1 whole chicken breast, boned and flattened to even thickness
2 chicken thighs, boned and flattened to even thickness
2 ounces prosciutto *or* pancetta, sliced ¼ inch thick
3 1-inch-thick slices day-old Italian bread (with crusts)
   Olive oil
   Freshly ground pepper
12 bay leaves, soaked in water 1 hour and torn in half crosswise
12 thin unpeeled lemon slices, halved

Anchovy Lemon Butter
½ cup (1 stick) unsalted butter
1 ounce anchovy fillets rolled with capers, drained, *or* 1 ounce anchovy fillets and 6 to 8 capers, drained
   Juice of ½ small lemon

Slice chicken breast into 12 even strips *(leave skin intact).* Slice each thigh into 6 chunks *(leave skin intact).* Slice prosciutto into 12 strips, rolling each strip into tight coil. Cut each slice of bread into 8 pieces. Rub each piece of chicken with olive oil and season with pepper. Roll chicken strips into tight coils. Thread ingredients onto 9- to 10-inch skewers in this order: bread, bay leaf, lemon, chicken breast, prosciutto, chicken thigh, lemon, bay leaf and bread. Brush skewers with olive oil. Refrigerate until ready to grill.
   For butter: Melt butter in small saucepan over low heat; keep warm. Mash anchovies and capers with fork in medium bowl until smooth. Gradually whisk in lemon juice, then whisk in melted butter 1 drop at a time.
   Prepare barbecue grill or preheat broiler. Grill skewers at least 4 inches from heat source until chicken is just tender and golden brown, about 12 to 15 minutes *(watch carefully so lemon and bay leaf do not burn).* Spoon butter sauce over skewers. Serve warm or at room temperature.

Lemon-Tarragon Chicken

By partially precooking chicken in the oven and then finishing it on the barbecue, we achieve the best of both worlds—it's evenly done with savory barbecue flavor. Oven cooking could be done 1 day ahead; let stand at room temperature 45 minutes before grilling.

4 servings

1 3- to 3½-pound chicken
1 large lemon, peeled (remove all white membrane), sliced very thinly and pitted
2 tablespoons loosely packed fresh tarragon leaves *or* 1½ teaspoons dried

Salt and freshly ground pepper

6 tablespoons (¾ stick) butter, melted
4 garlic cloves, minced

Preheat oven to 350°F. Place chicken breast side up on work surface. Carefully slip lemon slices under skin, covering breast, thigh and back as much as possible. Arrange tarragon leaves over lemon slices. Turn chicken over and make cut down length of backbone. Cut other side of backbone and remove. Turn breast side up and flatten by pressing on breastbone (remove breastbone if desired). Tuck legs toward breast; fold wings behind breast. Set chicken breast side up in shallow roasting pan and sprinkle with salt and pepper. Roast 45 minutes, basting occasionally with pan juices.

Heat coals in barbecue grill until gray ash forms. Spread around perimeter of barbecue so center is empty. Place drip pan in center. Set grill about 4 inches above coals and let coals burn about 20 minutes.

Set chicken breast side up in center of grill. Combine butter and garlic and brush chicken generously. Cook 15 to 20 minutes. Turn chicken over, brush generously with butter mixture and continue cooking until crisped and browned, about 15 to 20 minutes. Serve hot or at room temperature.

🍎 *Poached, Braised and Steamed*

Circassian Chicken (Cold Poached Chicken in Walnut Sauce)

The off-heat poaching method leaves chicken tender and succulent.

2 servings

4 cups water
1 medium carrot, cut into 1-inch pieces
½ medium onion, coarsely chopped
2 parsley sprigs
1 whole chicken breast (retain bone and skin)

⅔ cup (3 ounces) walnuts
1 slice firm white bread
1 tablespoon minced onion

Hungarian sweet paprika (garnish)

Combine water, carrot, onion and parsley in heavy medium saucepan. Cover and bring to boil over high heat. Remove from heat and add chicken breast. Cover and let stand at room temperature 2 hours.

Discard skin and bones from chicken (reserve broth). Halve meat lengthwise, then cut into small pieces crosswise, retaining shape of breast. Wrap in plastic and refrigerate.

Strain cooking liquid. Return to saucepan and boil over high heat until reduced to ½ cup, about 25 minutes. Mix walnuts, bread and minced onion in processor or blender. With machine running, slowly add reduced chicken broth and blend mixture thoroughly.

Transfer chicken to plate. Spread walnut sauce over. Sprinkle generously with paprika and serve immediately.

❦ Poaching Chicken Breasts

Chicken breasts can be poached either in butter or in a water-based liquid. Boned and skinned breasts (*suprêmes de volaille*) are poached in butter in order to baste the meat and seal in its juices. This simple, speedy procedure produces elegant results that are perfect party fare.

Poaching breasts in a liquid is the best way to cook chicken that is to be used in other dishes, such as soups and casseroles. It is the first step in the preparation of chicken salad and chicken sandwiches and any other recipe calling for cooked chicken.

Great Hints

- Poach chicken breasts in good quality, rich stock.
- Let breasts cool in stock to absorb as much flavor as possible.
- Reserve bones from butter- and liquid-poached breasts. Freeze and use to enrich chicken stock or soup.

Chicken Breasts Poached in Butter

Serve these with an herb butter, sautéed vegetables or a sauce, such as Cucumber-Dill Sauce (see recipe, page 109). This cooking method works equally well in the oven or on the stove. The suprêmes cook so rapidly that it's best to prepare their accompaniment first.

4 servings

4 chicken breast halves, skinned and boned, room temperature
¼ cup (½ stick) unsalted butter, melted
½ teaspoon paprika
¼ teaspoon minced fresh garlic *or* onion
Salt and freshly ground pepper
Fresh lemon juice

If using oven, preheat to 425°F. To ensure even cooking, gently pound chicken breasts between 2 pieces of plastic wrap or waxed paper until they are of equal thickness throughout. Dry thoroughly on paper towels. Season melted butter with paprika, garlic or onion and salt and pepper. Dip suprêmes in seasoned butter and sprinkle with lemon juice (*this keeps them white*). Transfer to nonstick skillet large enough to accommodate them in a single layer. Place buttered waxed paper or parchment over breasts and cover tightly with lid or foil. Bake, or cook on stove top over medium-high heat, until opaque and springy to the touch, about 8 to 10 minutes; *watch closely so they do not overcook (juices should run clear when meat is pierced).*

Chicken Breasts Poached in Water-Based Liquid

Poaching in a liquid is convenient when breasts are to be used to make other dishes, such as salads, sandwiches, crepes or casseroles, and meat can easily be boned after cooking.

Sticky Chicken

Freshly steamed rice is an excellent accompaniment.

4 to 6 servings

½ cup vinegar
½ cup sugar
½ cup soy sauce
4¼ pounds chicken pieces

2 garlic cloves, minced
1 tablespoon minced fresh ginger
Cherry tomatoes (garnish)
Watercress (garnish)

Combine vinegar, sugar and soy sauce in shallow baking dish. Arrange chicken in dish in single layer, turning to coat well. Cover and refrigerate overnight.

Transfer chicken and marinade to heavy large skillet. Add garlic and ginger and bring to boil over medium-high heat. Reduce heat, cover and simmer 15 minutes, turning occasionally. Uncover and continue simmering until chicken is tender and juices run clear when pricked with fork, about 15 minutes. Transfer chicken to heated platter. Cover with foil and keep warm in very low oven. Increase heat to medium and cook sauce until reduced and caramelized, about 25 minutes; *watch carefully to prevent burning.* Return chicken to skillet and coat with sauce. Garnish with cherry tomatoes and watercress. Serve hot.

Stuffed Chicken Breasts with Vegetable Sauce (Blanc de Volaille)

This light first course or entrée is topped with a rich Crème Fraîche–based sauce of fresh vegetables.

4 servings

2 3- to 3½-pound chickens

Stock
1 carrot, cut into chunks
1 medium onion, quartered
1 celery stalk (with leaves)
1 medium leek, including 2 inches of green, quartered
1 tomato, peeled (optional)
1 sprig tarragon
1 sprig thyme

Sauce
2 cups plus 2 tablespoons Crème Fraîche (see following recipe)

1 carrot, cut into very fine julienne slices
1 leek, trimmed and cut into very fine julienne slices

1 celery stalk, cut into very fine julienne slices
8 fresh morels* (*or* 4 large mushrooms, sliced horizontally into sixths), sautéed in 2 tablespoons (¼ stick) butter
2 snow peas, blanched and cut into fourths
Salt and freshly ground pepper

½ cup fine julienne of celery
½ cup fine julienne of leek
½ cup fine julienne of carrot
2 teaspoons chopped fresh chives

8 fresh morels*
4 teaspoons butter

Slit chickens along breastbone and peel off skin. Remove wishbone and cut off ½ breast for each serving. Set aside. Cut off legs (reserve for another use). Remove wings, crack and chop. Trim off excess fat. Crack carcasses with heavy knife.

For stock: Combine carcasses, wings, carrot, onion, celery, leek, tomato, tarragon and thyme in large saucepan and cover with water. Cover saucepan, place over medium heat and boil gently 30 to 60 minutes.

For sauce: Strain 3 cups stock into large saucepan, reserving remainder. Place over medium-high heat and bring to boil. Reduce heat and simmer until stock is reduced to 1½ cups. Add Crème Fraîche and continue cooking until mixture is reduced to 1½ cups.

Meanwhile, combine julienne of carrot, leek and celery stalk in strainer set

*Dried morels can be substituted for fresh. Combine in bowl with enough boiling water to cover. Let stand until softened. Drain well; pat dry with paper towels.

in pan of boiling water over medium-high heat. Blanch vegetables until crisp-tender, about 5 to 10 seconds. Plunge into ice water to stop cooking process. Drain and pat dry. Add to sauce with fresh morels and snow peas. Season with salt and pepper. Remove from heat and keep warm.

Form arc-shaped pocket in each chicken breast by slitting horizontally, leaving ½ inch at each end. Sprinkle all surfaces with salt and pepper. Combine ½ cup each celery, leek and carrot in strainer set in pan of boiling water over medium-high heat. Blanch until crisp-tender, about 5 to 10 seconds. Plunge into ice water to stop cooking process. Drain and pat dry. Transfer to medium bowl. Add chives and toss thoroughly.

Arrange 6 tablespoons vegetable mixture inside each chicken breast. Top each with 2 morels. Carefully close pocket and press edges to seal. Top each with 1 teaspoon butter. Wrap tightly in 10-inch piece of plastic wrap, twisting ends to seal. Transfer to shallow large saucepan. Strain enough reserved stock into saucepan to cover chicken. Bring to boil over medium-high heat. Reduce heat to medium and poach chicken about 8 to 10 minutes, turning carefully once or twice. Remove chicken from pan using slotted spoon and let drain.

Divide sauce evenly among plates. Unwrap 1 breast, slice diagonally into 4 pieces and arrange on plate in pinwheel pattern. Repeat with remaining breasts. Serve immediately.

Crème Fraîche

Combine 1 part sour cream and 2 parts whipping cream. Heat to 110°F, then let stand at room temperature until thick, about 8 hours.

Chèvre and Mushroom-stuffed Chicken Legs

6 servings

5 ounces fresh goat cheese, such as Bûcheron or Montrachet
4 thin slices salami, minced
2 tablespoons minced green onion *or* minced fresh chives
1 teaspoon minced fresh parsley

6 large chicken legs with thighs attached

6 dried morel mushrooms
1 heaping tablespoon dried cèpes *or* porcini mushrooms

3 tablespoons unsalted butter

1 tablespoon vegetable oil
½ cup minced shallot
1 garlic clove, minced
2 tablespoons Sherry vinegar
4 cups rich homemade unsalted chicken stock, reduced to 2 cups
¼ teaspoon fresh thyme leaves *or* pinch of dried
Salt and freshly ground pepper

1 teaspoon fresh tarragon *or* ¼ teaspoon dried
2 tablespoons tomato puree

Blend cheese, salami, onion and parsley in small bowl. *(Can be prepared up to 3 days ahead and refrigerated.)*

To bone chicken, place 1 chicken leg skin side down on work surface. Make slit along side of thighbone, continuing slit down center of drumstick. Holding hip end of thigh in one hand, gradually release thigh by scraping meat off bone on all sides. Remove thigh by cutting through socket where it articulates with drumstick, being careful to avoid piercing skin. Cut around head of drumstick to free it, then bone out completely according to instructions for thigh. Cut out cartilage, again not piercing skin. Remove each tendon by holding onto end and scraping off meat as you pull it out. Arrange boned leg meat side up. Repeat with remaining chicken legs.

Divide stuffing among chicken legs. Fold over sides to close completely. Sew edges together using thick cotton thread and long needle.

Rinse all dried mushrooms under cold water. Transfer to small bowl. Cover with hot water and let soften 40 minutes. Rinse morels inside and out to remove sand; slice thinly. Remove cèpes, squeezing dry (reserve soaking liquid); chop. Strain liquid through sieve lined with dampened paper towel; set liquid aside.

Heat 1 tablespoon butter with oil in heavy nonaluminum large skillet over medium-high heat. Add half of chicken and brown on all sides, turning with wooden spatula to avoid piercing skin. Drain thoroughly on paper towels. Repeat with remaining chicken.

Pour off all fat from skillet. Melt remaining 2 tablespoons butter in same skillet over medium heat. Add shallot and stir until soft, 2 to 3 minutes. Stir in garlic and mushrooms and cook until aromatic, about 1 minute. Add vinegar and reduce to glaze, scraping up any browned bits. Pour in reserved soaking liquid and reduce by about half. Add stock, thyme and salt and pepper. Arrange chicken legs in skillet seam side up. Bring liquid to gentle simmer. Cover and cook until ends of thighs are firm, about 25 minutes.

Transfer chicken to platter. Degrease sauce. Add tarragon and bring to boil. Cook until thickened and reduced by about ⅔. Meanwhile, remove thread from chickens. Stir tomato puree into sauce. Adjust seasoning. Pour sauce over chicken and serve immediately.

Coq au Riesling

Cooked in the aromatic white wine of Alsace, this dish is lighter and more delicate than the better known coq au vin rouge from Burgundy. Be sure to use a white wine that is not too acidic. Boiled potatoes or homemade noodles are a good accompaniment.

4 servings

1 3- to 3½-pound chicken, quartered
   Salt and freshly ground pepper
5 tablespoons butter
2 tablespoons oil
4 shallots, chopped
1½ tablespoons Cognac
1½ cups dry white wine (preferably Alsatian Riesling)
   Bouquet garni (thyme, bay leaf and parsley tied in a cheesecloth bag)

   Salt and freshly ground pepper
   Pinch of freshly grated nutmeg

5 ounces fresh button mushrooms, quartered
3 tablespoons fresh lemon juice or to taste

⅓ cup whipping cream
1 egg yolk

Season chicken with salt and pepper. Heat 3 tablespoons butter with oil in large pot or Dutch oven over medium-high heat. Add chicken and brown on all sides. Reduce heat, add shallots and continue cooking 2 minutes. Drain off all fat. Add Cognac and ignite, shaking pot until flame dies. Stir chicken quickly and add wine, bouquet garni, salt and pepper and nutmeg. Bring to boil, then cover and simmer until chicken is almost tender, 40 to 50 minutes.

About 5 minutes before chicken is done, melt remaining 2 tablespoons butter in small skillet over low heat. Add mushrooms and lemon juice and cook until tender. Add to chicken.

Remove from heat and discard bouquet garni. Transfer chicken and mushrooms to heated serving platter. Mix cream with yolk in small bowl. Slowly add cooking liquid, beating constantly until sauce is creamy. Strain directly over chicken and serve immediately.

Creamy Paprika Chicken

6 servings

6 tablespoons (¾ stick) butter
2 large chickens (about 6 pounds total), cut into serving pieces and patted dry
4 large onions, chopped
3 to 4 tablespoons Hungarian sweet paprika
4 large tomatoes, coarsely chopped

2 green bell peppers, seeded, deveined and sliced
4 to 6 tablespoons sour cream, room temperature
¼ cup whipping cream, room temperature
Salt and freshly ground pepper

Melt butter in heavy deep skillet over medium-high heat. Add chicken in batches and brown on all sides. Remove chicken and set aside. Add onions and paprika to skillet; cover and cook, stirring occasionally, until onion is soft but not browned, about 10 minutes. Stir in tomatoes and green peppers. Arrange chicken over top. Reduce heat to low, cover and simmer until chicken is cooked through, about 20 minutes *(if tomatoes exude liquid and sauce seems thin, set chicken aside and reduce sauce over medium-high heat to desired consistency before proceeding).* Stir in sour cream and whipping cream. Season with salt and freshly ground pepper. Serve immediately.

Chicken in Silky Almond Sauce
(Murghi dil Bahasht)

8 servings

2 3- to 3½-pound chickens, each cut into 8 pieces and skinned (do not use wing tips)
2 tablespoons vegetable oil

½ cup vegetable oil
5 cups thinly sliced onion (about 5 medium)
6 tablespoons blanched slivered *or* ground almonds
3 tablespoons ground coriander

2 tablespoons chopped fresh ginger
2 teaspoons ground cardamom
2 teaspoons ground red pepper
1 teaspoon ground cumin
½ teaspoon ground fennel seed

2 cups plain yogurt
1 cup water
Coarse salt
Fresh cilantro (coriander) (garnish)

Pat chicken dry. Heat 2 tablespoons oil in heavy-bottomed large skillet or Dutch oven over medium-high heat. Add chicken in batches and cook on all sides just until no longer pink *(do not brown).* Remove using slotted spoon and set aside.

Heat remaining oil in skillet. Add sliced onion and fry until wilted and pale brown, stirring constantly to color evenly, about 12 minutes. Stir in almonds, coriander, ginger, cardamom, ground red pepper, cumin and fennel and cook 3 to 5 more minutes. Remove mixture from heat.

Transfer half of mixture to processor or blender. Puree with 1 cup yogurt and ½ cup water. Repeat with remaining onion mixture, yogurt and water. Pour almond sauce back into skillet. Add chicken to skillet. Place over medium-high heat and bring to boil. Reduce heat, cover and simmer until chicken is tender and sauce is thickened, about 45 minutes *(oil will begin to separate from sauce and thin glaze will form over chicken).* Remove from heat. Season with salt. Let stand at room temperature at least 30 minutes (preferably 1 hour, or refrigerate overnight). Rewarm over very low heat. Transfer to serving dish. Garnish with cilantro and serve immediately.

Tangier Tajine

8 servings

3 tablespoons vegetable oil
8 chicken legs with thighs attached
2 cups water
2 garlic cloves, crushed
¼ teaspoon cinnamon
¼ teaspoon freshly grated nutmeg
Salt and freshly ground pepper

1 cup pitted prunes
½ cup slivered almonds

Freshly steamed couscous
¼ cup slivered almonds, toasted (garnish)

Preheat oven to 350°F. Heat oil in heavy large skillet over medium-high heat. Add chicken and brown well on all sides. Transfer to casserole or Dutch oven. Pour off excess oil from skillet. Add 1 cup water and stir, scraping up any browned bits clinging to bottom of pan. Pour over chicken. Stir in garlic, cinnamon, nutmeg and salt and pepper. Add remaining water and blend well.

Cover and bake until chicken is almost tender, about 15 minutes. Add prunes and ½ cup almonds and continue baking until chicken is cooked through, about 15 minutes.

Spread freshly steamed couscous on large platter. Top with chicken and sauce. Sprinkle with almonds.

Chicken One-Pot with Dumplings (Hühnertopf mit Klösschen)

4 to 5 servings

Chicken
2 medium leeks, trimmed (reserve green tops)
2 tablespoons (¼ stick) butter
¼ cup chopped fresh parsley
1 tablespoon diced celery root *or* chopped celery, including leaves
5 cups water
1 3- to 3½-pound chicken, split in half

4 medium carrots, coarsely sliced
2 medium turnips, peeled and coarsely cubed
2½ cups coarsely sliced cauliflower florets

1 cup firm cabbage chunks
1 teaspoon salt
¼ teaspoon freshly ground pepper

Dumplings
⅔ cup milk
2 tablespoons (¼ stick) butter
½ teaspoon salt
Pinch of freshly grated nutmeg
1 cup all purpose flour
4 tablespoons chopped fresh parsley
1 egg, beaten

For chicken: Halve leek greens lengthwise and chop. Cut white part into ¾-inch slices. Melt butter in large Dutch oven or flameproof casserole over medium heat. Add leek greens, parsley and celery root and cook, stirring constantly until vegetables are limp, about 4 to 5 minutes. Add water and chicken. Cover and bring to boil. Reduce heat and simmer until chicken is just tender, about 1¾ hours.

Transfer chicken to platter and let cool. Discard any fat from broth. Layer carrots, turnips and sliced leeks in broth. Top with cauliflower and cabbage. Add salt and pepper. Cover and simmer over low heat 20 minutes. Remove chicken from bones and cut meat into bite-size pieces. Add to vegetables and continue cooking until carrots are tender, about 10 to 15 minutes.

Meanwhile, prepare dumplings: Combine milk, butter, salt and nutmeg in small saucepan over medium heat. Cook until butter is melted and milk is very hot *(do not allow to boil)*. Remove from heat. Add flour and 2 tablespoons parsley, stirring dough vigorously until well blended. Add egg, beating vigorously.

Drain broth from Dutch oven into large saucepan. Place pan over high heat and bring to boil. Form dough into walnut-size dumplings using 2 teaspoons. Add to broth in batches and cook 6 to 7 minutes; as dumplings rise to surface, add to chicken using slotted spoon. Adjust seasoning of broth and pour over chicken and dumplings. Reheat until piping hot. Transfer to soup tureen or serve from Dutch oven. Sprinkle with remaining 2 tablespoons parsley and serve immediately.

Chicken-Raviolini Stew

4 servings

12 chicken wings (about 2½ pounds), wing tips removed if desired
3 celery stalks, trimmed and sliced (about 1 cup)
1 medium onion, minced (about 1 cup)
1 bay leaf

1 teaspoon dried basil
½ teaspoon dried sage
Salt and freshly ground pepper
12 1-inch cheese raviolini,* cooked and drained
¼ cup freshly grated Parmesan cheese

Place chicken wings in 6-quart saucepan with enough water to cover by 1 inch. Add celery, onion, bay leaf, basil, sage and salt and pepper and bring to boil over medium-high heat. Reduce heat to low, cover and simmer 25 minutes. Divide chicken wings and raviolini evenly among 4 large soup bowls. Skim fat from surface of broth and strain into bowls. Sprinkle each with cheese and serve.

*Available in Italian markets.

Chinatown Restaurant
Steamed Chicken in Lotus Leaf

If a lotus leaf is not available, leek leaves are a savory substitute.

4 to 6 servings

2 tablespoons light soy sauce
1 4-pound chicken

1 large lotus leaf *or* 3 to 4 large leek leaves

2 teaspoons cornstarch mixed with ½ cup water
¼ pound lean pork, cut into ¼-inch cubes

8 to 9 cups oil (for deep frying)

8 shallots, chopped
8 garlic cloves, chopped
4 dried oriental black mushrooms, soaked 30 minutes in warm water, drained, stems discarded and caps shredded

3½ ounces preserved Yunan turnip* (also known as Yunan vegetable or Yunan cabbage), shredded
⅓ cup shredded onion
¼ cup bamboo shoots, sliced and shredded
1½ teaspoons rice wine *or* dry Sherry
Oyster Sesame Sauce (see following recipe)
1 tablespoon tiny green peas

Rub 2 tablespoons light soy sauce evenly over chicken and inside cavity.

Combine lotus leaf in large pot with enough water to cover. Place over medium-high heat and bring to boil. Let boil until lotus leaf is soft, about 3 minutes. Drain well; transfer to bowl of cool water and set aside. (If leek leaves are used, blanch in boiling water until pliable, about 3 to 5 minutes. Drain on paper towels.)

Sprinkle cornstarch mixture over pork and mix well. Set aside.

Heat oil in wok or deep pot to 350°F. Slowly lower chicken into oil, breast side down, and deep fry until golden brown, turning chicken as necessary for even browning. Carefully remove chicken from wok using large tongs. Let chicken drain on paper towels.

Carefully pour off oil from wok, reserving 2 tablespoons. Heat reserved oil over medium-high heat. Add shallots and garlic and sauté until lightly golden. Add mushrooms, turnip, onion, bamboo shoots and pork and stir-fry about 5 minutes. Blend in the rice wine. Stir Oyster Sesame Sauce through several times and add to wok. Bring mixture to boil, reduce heat to medium low and add green peas. Simmer uncovered about 3 minutes. Transfer mixture to bowl and let cool.

Spoon mixture into cavity of chicken. Carefully wrap lotus leaf around chicken. Set breast side up on plate. Add 1 inch water to deep large pot. Set steamer inside (or use rack that will hold chicken above water). Set chicken on plate in steamer. Bring water to boil over medium-high heat. Reduce heat, cover tightly and steam chicken over simmering water until tender, about 2 hours. Transfer chicken to platter, reserving accumulated liquid. To serve, crosscut lotus leaf and peel back to reveal chicken. Pour liquid accumulated during steaming over chicken.

* Available in oriental markets.

Oyster Sesame Sauce

Makes about ⅓ cup

3 tablespoons chicken stock *or* water
2 teaspoons oyster sauce*
1½ teaspoons cornstarch
1 teaspoon salt

1 teaspoon sugar
1 teaspoon light soy sauce
1 teaspoon sesame oil*
½ teaspoon dark soy sauce
Freshly ground pepper

Combine ingredients and mix well.

* Available in oriental markets.

Pepper-steamed Chicken with Roasted Onion Sauce

6 servings

1 teaspoon black peppercorns, crushed
6 chicken breast halves, boned and skinned
3 to 4 tablespoons fresh lemon juice
3 medium onions, unpeeled
1 tablespoon Spanish Sherry vinegar
1 teaspoon butter (optional)

Salt and freshly ground pepper

4 cups water
2 whole cloves
1 small onion, sliced
1 lemon, peeled, seeded and chopped
1 tablespoon ground cardamom

Minced fresh parsley (garnish)

Rub half of crushed peppercorns into both sides of each chicken breast. Transfer chicken to shallow baking dish and sprinkle with lemon juice. Cover and refrigerate 8 to 10 hours.

Position rack in center of oven and preheat to 425°F. Rinse onions and place on piece of heavy-duty aluminum foil. Roast onions until easily pierced with knife, about 1¼ hours. *(Onions can be prepared 1 or 2 days ahead.)* Trim off stem, root ends and first layer of onion peel. Transfer onions to processor or blender in batches. Add vinegar and butter and puree until smooth. Season with salt and pepper and set aside.

Just before serving, drain chicken well. Combine 4 cups water with cloves, onion, lemon, cardamom and remaining peppercorns in large saucepan with steamer rack. Cover and bring to boil over medium-high heat. Let boil 5 minutes. Arrange chicken breasts in single layer on steamer rack *(do not allow liquid to touch chicken)*. Cover and steam until chicken is slightly firm, about 7 minutes.

Meanwhile, transfer onion sauce to small saucepan over medium heat and cook just until heated through. Transfer chicken breasts to 6 heated plates and nap with some of sauce. Garnish with parsley and serve immediately. Pass additional sauce separately.

Cold Lemon Chicken

6 to 8 servings

5 chicken breast halves

10 dried black mushrooms, soaked in boiling water 30 minutes

2 tablespoons vegetable oil

¼ cup fresh ginger cut into julienne slices

¼ cup red *or* green chili peppers cut julienne *or* ½ teaspoon chili paste with garlic*

¼ cup lemon peel cut into julienne slices

2 tablespoons sugar

½ cup fresh lemon juice
Salt

1 tablespoon finely grated lemon peel

2 teaspoons lemon extract

Pour about 2 inches water in steamer and bring to boil. Set chicken in bowl, place on rack in steamer, cover and cook until tender, about 1 hour. Let cool in broth. Discard skin and bones; cut meat into 1-inch cubes. Strain broth into 1-cup measure and set aside.

Drain mushroom liquid into broth if necessary to make 1 cup total; squeeze mushrooms dry. Remove stems and slice caps into thin shreds.

Heat oil in wok over medium-high heat. Add ginger and shredded mushrooms and stir-fry 1 minute. Add peppers or chili paste, lemon peel and sugar and stir well. Add chicken broth and bring to boil. Add lemon juice and mix well. Season with salt to taste.

Add chicken and stir for 30 seconds. Transfer to serving dish. Blend grated peel and extract into sauce, stir well and pour over chicken. Serve either at room temperature or chilled.

*Available in oriental markets.

❦ Sautéed

Chicken Sauté with Mushrooms, Shallots and Herbs

4 servings

1 3- to 3½-pound chicken, cut into 9 pieces
Salt and freshly ground pepper
1 tablespoon vegetable oil
1 tablespoon butter
¼ pound mushrooms, sliced

4 teaspoons finely minced shallot

½ cup dry white wine
⅔ cup Tomato-flavored Brown Sauce (see following recipe)

4 teaspoons Cognac
2 teaspoons chopped fresh tarragon *or* 1½ teaspoon dried
2 teaspoons chopped fresh parsley (garnish)

Pat chicken dry. Sprinkle lightly on all sides with salt and pepper. Heat oil with butter in heavy large skillet over medium-high heat. Add chicken pieces (in batches if necessary) and brown thoroughly on all sides; *do not crowd*. Transfer to plate using slotted spoon. Add mushrooms to skillet and brown.

Reduce heat to low. Return all chicken to skillet with juices remaining on plate. Cover and simmer until breast pieces are tender, about 15 minutes.

Transfer breast pieces to platter using slotted spoon. Cover and keep warm. Add shallot to skillet. Continue cooking remaining chicken until tender, about 10 minutes. Transfer to same platter, leaving vegetables in skillet.

Skim off as much fat as possible from mixture in skillet. Reheat until very hot. Pour in wine and bring to boil. Let boil, stirring and skimming frequently, until reduced by about half. Reduce heat to medium, add brown sauce and 2 teaspoons Cognac and continue simmering, stirring frequently, until sauce is thick enough to coat spoon. Stir in tarragon and remaining Cognac. Adjust seasoning. Spoon mushrooms and sauce over chicken. Top with parsley and serve.

Tomato-flavored Brown Sauce

Sauce can be prepared ahead and in larger quantities to be used in recipes that call for brown sauce. Store in refrigerator several days or freeze.

Makes ⅔ cup

2 teaspoons vegetable oil
Wing tips and neck of 1 chicken, chopped into several pieces
½ onion, diced
½ carrot, diced
1 cup chicken stock
2 fresh tomatoes *or* canned plum tomatoes, coarsely chopped

Pinch of dried thyme
½ small bay leaf

2 tablespoons cold water
1 teaspoon tomato paste
1 teaspoon potato starch, arrowroot *or* cornstarch

Heat oil in heavy medium saucepan over medium-high heat. Add wing tips, neck, onion and carrot and sauté just until well browned. Stir in stock, tomatoes, thyme and bay leaf. Bring to boil, stirring constantly. Reduce heat to very low and simmer uncovered about 45 minutes.

Strain stock into another medium saucepan, pressing on vegetables to extract all liquid. Skim as much fat as possible from surface. Simmer over medium heat until reduced to ⅔ cup. Blend cold water into tomato paste in small bowl. Add potato starch and whisk to form smooth paste. Gradually whisk mixture into simmering sauce. Return to boil, whisking constantly until thickened. Remove from heat and serve.

Chicken Sauté with Red Wine

4 servings

½ pound thickly sliced bacon, cut crosswise into ¼-inch strips
24 uniform-size pearl onions, peeled
2 tablespoons (¼ stick) butter, room temperature
½ pound mushrooms, quartered
Salt and freshly ground pepper

1 3- to 3½-pound chicken, cut into 9 pieces

3 tablespoons butter
4 teaspoons all purpose flour

2 garlic cloves, minced
2 cups dry red wine
1⅓ cups chicken stock

Large pinch of sugar (optional)

Cook bacon in heavy large skillet over medium-low heat until fat begins to render. Increase heat to medium high, add onions and sauté until bacon is brown. Transfer bacon to paper towels using slotted spoon. Continue to sauté onions, turning carefully, until browned on all sides, about 5 more minutes. Transfer onions to paper towels. Discard all but 1 tablespoon fat from skillet. Add 1 tablespoon butter and melt over medium heat. Add mushrooms and salt and pepper and brown lightly. Transfer to paper towels using slotted spoon.

Pat chicken dry. Sprinkle lightly on all sides with salt and pepper. Melt 1 tablespoon butter in same skillet over medium-high heat. Add chicken pieces (in batches if necessary) and brown thoroughly on all sides; *do not crowd*. Return legs, thighs and onions to skillet. Scatter mushrooms over top. Arrange breast and wing pieces over mushrooms. Pour juices remaining on plate over chicken. Reduce heat to low, cover and cook gently until breast pieces are tender when pierced.

Meanwhile, mash remaining 3 tablespoons butter in cup. Add flour and mix to form paste.

Transfer breast pieces to platter using slotted spoon. Cover and keep warm. Continue cooking remaining chicken and vegetables until tender, about 10 minutes. Using slotted spoon, transfer mushrooms and onions to medium bowl. Add drained bacon.

Skim off as much fat as possible from juices in skillet. Reheat juices until very hot, scraping up any browned bits. Add garlic to skillet and stir over low heat 30 seconds. Pour in wine and bring to boil. Let boil 3 minutes. Add stock and boil, stirring and skimming fat frequently, until sauce is reduced to about 1½ cups. Pour sauce into heavy medium saucepan and bring to simmer. Gradually add butter mixture to simmering sauce, whisking constantly, then bring to boil, continuing to whisk.

Return vegetable-bacon mixture to sauce. Reduce heat to low and cook 2 minutes to blend flavors. Adjust seasoning; if flavor is too tart, add pinch of sugar. Spoon sauce and vegetable-bacon mixture over chicken and serve.

Chicken Sauté with Asparagus and Carrots

This colorful spring dish contains a generous amount of vegetables.

4 servings

1 3- to 3½-pound chicken, cut into 9 pieces
Salt and freshly ground pepper
1 tablespoon vegetable oil
1 tablespoon butter

3 medium carrots, peeled and thickly sliced or cut into nuggets

1 bunch (about 1¼ pounds) asparagus, peeled and trimmed

½ cup Madeira
½ cup whipping cream

Poached leek strips

Pat chicken dry. Sprinkle lightly on all sides with salt and pepper. Heat oil with butter in heavy 12-inch skillet over medium-high heat. Add chicken (in batches if necessary) and brown lightly on all sides, about 10 minutes; *do not crowd.* Transfer each piece to plate as it browns using slotted spoon.

Return all chicken to skillet with juices remaining on plate. Reduce heat to low; cover and simmer until breast pieces are tender, about 15 minutes.

Transfer breast pieces to platter. Cover and keep warm. Continue cooking remaining chicken until tender, about 5 minutes. Place on platter.

While chicken is cooking, place carrots in medium saucepan. Cover with water and season with salt. Bring to boil. Reduce heat, cover and simmer until barely tender, 15 to 20 minutes.

Meanwhile, cut off asparagus tips. Halve stems crosswise, then halve stems lengthwise as necessary to same thickness as carrots. Add stems to carrots and continue simmering until tender, about 4 minutes. Transfer all vegetables to medium skillet; set aside. Reserve 1 cup cooking liquid.

Skim off as much fat as possible from juices in skillet. Reheat juices until very hot, scraping up any browned bits. Add reserved vegetable cooking liquid to skillet and boil, stirring frequently, until reduced to ¼ cup, about 10 minutes. Add Madeira and return to boil. Reduce heat to medium. Add cream and simmer, stirring frequently, until thick enough to coat spoon, about 7 minutes. Taste and adjust seasoning. Reheat vegetables in medium skillet over medium-high heat. Blanch asparagus tips.

Drain any fat from platter; wipe clean. Spoon carrots and the asparagus stems onto platter. Tie asparagus tips in bundles using leek strips (see photograph). Arrange around chicken. Top chicken with sauce.

Chicken Sauté with Oranges and Avocados

Offer a simple spinach salad, dessert—a spoon bread, perhaps—and a dry California Chenin Blanc.

6 servings

6 chicken breast halves, boned and skinned
All purpose flour
3 tablespoons butter
2 tablespoons safflower oil
¾ cup fresh orange juice
⅓ cup dry white wine
⅓ cup sliced mushrooms
2 tablespoons minced fresh parsley

1 teaspoon finely grated orange peel
Pinch of dried rosemary
3 tablespoons raspberry vinegar
2 oranges, peeled, sectioned and seeded (garnish)
2 avocados, peeled, pitted and sliced (garnish)

Pound chicken slightly to flatten to even thickness. Dredge lightly in flour, shaking off excess. Heat butter with oil in heavy large skillet over medium-high heat. Add chicken (in batches if necessary) and sauté on both sides until well browned. Add orange juice, wine, mushrooms, parsley, orange peel and rosemary and bring to simmer. Let simmer 5 minutes. Transfer chicken to heated serving platter using slotted spoon. Add vinegar to skillet and continue simmering, scraping up any browned bits, until sauce is reduced by about ⅓. Pour sauce over chicken. Garnish with orange sections and avocado slices. Serve immediately.

Chicken with Raspberry Vinegar Sauce

3 to 4 servings

3 tablespoons butter
1 tablespoon oil
1 2½- to 3-pound chicken, cut into serving pieces
¾ teaspoon salt

¾ cup raspberry vinegar

1¼ cups rich chicken stock

1¼ cups whipping cream
Raspberry vinegar
Salt and freshly ground pepper

Heat butter with oil in large skillet. Add chicken and sauté on all sides until golden brown. Remove from skillet using tongs and sprinkle with salt; set aside.

Drain off excess fat and return skillet to heat. Deglaze pan by adding ¾ cup raspberry vinegar. Return chicken to pan, add stock and simmer, covered, until chicken is tender and juices run clear when pricked with a fork. Transfer chicken to serving platter and keep warm.

Bring liquid in pan to boil, then reduce heat and cook until sauce is consistency of light cream. Add cream and reduce sauce again. Add vinegar and salt and pepper to taste. Stir in juices that have accumulated on platter. Pour over chicken and serve immediately.

Chicken in Piquant Liver Sauce
(Pollo con Salsa di Fegato)

12 servings

11 to 13 tablespoons olive oil
24 chicken thighs

½ cup chopped onion
3 garlic cloves
4 chicken livers
4 chicken hearts
40 small capers
16 pitted green olives
5 anchovy fillets
2 tablespoons chopped fresh parsley

2 bay leaves
¼ teaspoon dried sage
Dash of freshly ground white pepper
1 tablespoon plus 1 teaspoon red wine vinegar
1 tablespoon plus 1 teaspoon fresh lemon juice

½ cup whipping cream, or more
Salt

Heat 2 tablespoons olive oil in each of 2 heavy large skillets over medium-high heat. Pat chicken dry. Add chicken to skillets and brown on both sides. Reduce heat, cover and cook until juices run clear when pierced with fork, about 20 minutes. *(Chicken can be prepared ahead. Cook only 15 minutes. Transfer to baking dishes in single layer. Cover with foil and set aside. Rewarm in 325°F oven about 20 minutes.)*

Meanwhile, heat 5 tablespoons olive oil in heavy medium skillet over low heat. Add onion and garlic, cover and cook until onion is translucent, about 10 minutes, stirring occasionally. Dry chicken livers and hearts. Add to skillet, increase heat to medium high and cook until giblets are browned on outside, about 3 minutes, stirring occasionally. Blend in capers, olives, anchovies, parsley, bay leaves, sage and white pepper and cook 3 minutes, stirring occasionally. Stir in vinegar and lemon juice and cook 2 minutes.

Discard bay leaves. Transfer liver mixture to processor using slotted spoon and blend to smooth paste using on/off turns, stopping to scrape down sides of work bowl, or whirl in blender in batches. Return mixture to skillet and blend with juices remaining in skillet. *(Sauce can be prepared several hours ahead to this point. Rewarm sauce over medium heat, whisking in small amount of cream to thin to desired consistency and recombine if separated.)* Place skillet over low heat and gradually stir in ½ cup cream, adding slightly more if sauce is too thick. Stir in remaining oil as desired. Season with salt.

Arrange chicken on platter. Spoon sauce over and serve immediately.

Poulet Sauté à la Bordelaise

2 servings

5 tablespoons butter
1 tablespoon olive oil
2 chicken legs
2 chicken thighs
   Salt and freshly ground pepper

1 artichoke, top cut off and leaves trimmed *or* ½ package frozen artichoke hearts, prepared according to package directions

1 small garlic clove, minced
½ cup rich chicken stock
½ cup dry white wine
1 teaspoon glace de viande (meat glaze)*

1 tablespoon tomato paste

1 medium potato

   Oil (for deep frying)
1 onion, thinly sliced and separated into rings
   Milk
   All purpose flour

   Parsley sprigs (garnish)

Heat 2 tablespoons butter with olive oil in heavy large skillet over medium-high heat. Add chicken and brown well on all sides. Sprinkle with salt and pepper. Reduce heat to low, cover and cook until tender, about 45 minutes.

Meanwhile, if using fresh artichoke, bring large saucepan of water to boil over high heat. Add artichoke, reduce heat and simmer until artichoke is tender, about 35 minutes. Drain well. Discard choke. Cut into quarters.

Remove chicken from skillet and keep warm. Heat drippings over medium-high heat. Add garlic and cook briefly. Stir in chicken stock, wine and meat glaze and cook, scraping up any browned bits clinging to bottom of skillet, until sauce is slightly thickened and reduced. Strain. Return sauce to skillet and stir in tomato paste. Cook until heated through. Season to taste with salt and pepper. Set aside and keep warm.

Melt 1 tablespoon butter in medium skillet over medium heat. Add artichoke and sauté until lightly browned. Set aside and keep warm. Peel potato and slice thinly; pat dry with paper towel. Melt remaining 2 tablespoons butter in same skillet over medium heat. Add potatoes and sauté until tender and lightly browned. Set aside and keep warm.

Pour frying oil into heavy large saucepan to depth of 2 inches and heat to 375°F. Dip onion into milk, then coat with flour, shaking off excess. Fry in batches until golden, about 2 to 3 minutes. Drain on paper towels.

Arrange chicken in center of heated platter and spoon sauce over. Ring with potatoes and onions. Garnish with artichokes and parsley sprigs.

*Available in specialty food stores.

❦ Suprêmes de Volaille

The *suprême de volaille,* or half a chicken breast that has been skinned, boned and pounded, has long been prized for its tenderness, delicate flavor and great versatility. Suprêmes are among the staples of cuisine, capable of being dressed up or down at the whim of the cook—they can be sautéed and sauced simply with cream and herbs or wine and lemon juice; they can also become the focus of a special dinner when stuffed with cheese or chicken liver pâté, or shaped into dainty *paupiettes,* or rolled around such fillings as frozen herb butter or slices of ham and cheese.

Suprêmes can also be the mainstay of the busy hostess. A wise cook will always have several of them stacked in the freezer as a hedge against unexpected guests. Their value as a last-minute entrée is further enhanced by the fact that they cook to tender, juicy perfection in 10 minutes or less.

Each suprême has 2 filets. They can be used separately or together; 6 of the small filets usually add up to 1 serving. If you prefer to leave the small filet mignon attached, tuck it under the boned larger filet before flattening.

Boning

This technique takes only 2 or 3 minutes and can be applied to either a whole chicken breast or a breast half. The boning process will be easier if the chicken has been placed in the freezer 30 to 60 minutes before you begin, and if the knife is very sharp.

1. Place breast on working surface skin side up. Starting at rib end, insert tip of sharp knife (preferably a boning knife) between rib cage and meat. Keeping knife as close to rib cage as possible, work it along edge of breast to other end, separating meat from bone and gristle to a depth of about 2 inches.

2. Using knife and/or fingers, scrape or push meat toward center breastbone until it is completely loosened from rib cage but still attached to center bone. If you are boning a whole breast, turn it around and repeat the process on the other side. With point of knife, work around wishbone (or segment of wishbone, if boning a breast half) to loosen. Remove wishbone.

3. Scrape or push meat away from center bone, being careful not to tear meat. Remove breastbone.

4. Peel off skin, using knife if necessary to avoid tearing meat, and trim off any bits of skin or fat that remain. To remove white tendons running along underside of breast, slip point of knife under one end of tendon to lift it away from meat, then hold end of tendon with one hand while carefully scraping meat from tendon.

Slice whole boned breast in half to form suprêmes, if desired.

If you do not plan to use meat immediately, wrap in plastic to prevent it from drying out.

Pounding

Pounding chicken breasts to a uniform thickness ensures quick and even cooking. If breasts are to be shaped into paupiettes or rolled around a filling, they must be pounded to a thickness of about ¼ inch.

A flat metal pounder is the ideal tool, but a number of common kitchen implements will do the job as well—try the flat side of a cleaver or a rolling pin. *(Do not use a meat-tenderizing mallet, since the teeth will damage the delicate meat.)*

Place boned and skinned breast between two pieces of waxed paper, skinned side up. Pound with even strokes until meat is about ¼ inch thick.

Filling and Rolling

Place suprême on board skinned side down. Arrange filling on one end, leaving room to fold sides over. Tuck in sides, then roll suprême into jelly roll shape. Meat is very pliable and can be pinched closed if necessary to cover any exposed filling.

Short and Sweet Ginger Chicken Breasts

4 servings

4 tablespoons (½ stick) butter, melted	8 8-ounce chicken breast halves, boned, skinned and pounded
4 tablespoons ginger marmalade Salt to taste	1 cup finely chopped nuts

Preheat oven to 350°F. Lightly grease a small roasting pan. Combine butter, marmalade and salt in blender or processor equipped with Steel Knife. Paint both sides of breasts with marmalade mixture. Dip into nuts and roll lengthwise into jelly roll shapes *(paupiettes)*. Bake seam side down in prepared pan tented with foil, 20 minutes. Remove foil and continue baking until breasts are cooked through, about 10 minutes. *Do not overbake.* To test for doneness, insert point of knife into underside of one of the rolls; meat should be white.

Stuffing

Place boned, skinned chicken breast on working surface, skinned side up *(do not pound)*. Holding breast securely with one hand, insert tip of boning knife into thickest part of breast and make a slit that runs about ⅔ the length of the breast, 1 to 1½ inches deep, depending on width of breast. Fill with any stuffing you choose and press edges together to seal. To make chicken easier to work with, place in freezer for about 30 minutes before stuffing.

Chicken-stuffed Palacsinta with Hungarian Paprika and Sour Cream

For best texture, spoon sauce over filled pancakes at the last minute.

6 servings

Palacsinta
- 1 cup milk
- 2 eggs
- ½ teaspoon Hungarian sweet *or* semisweet paprika
- ¼ teaspoon salt
- ¾ cup sifted all purpose flour
- 2 tablespoons (¼ stick) butter, melted
- 2 tablespoons chopped fresh parsley

  Vegetable oil

Filling and Sauce
- 3 tablespoons bacon fat *or* vegetable oil
- 4 chicken breast halves
- 2 large onions, coarsely chopped (about 3½ cups)
- 2 carrots, halved lengthwise and sliced
- 1 large green bell pepper *or* 1 small red and 1 small green bell pepper, cored, seeded and diced
- 1 celery stalk, sliced
- 2 to 3 garlic cloves, minced
- 3 to 4 tablespoons Hungarian semisweet paprika*
- 2 medium tomatoes, peeled, seeded and chopped *or* ⅔ cup tomato puree
- 1¼ cups strong chicken stock (preferably homemade)
  Pinch of dried marjoram

  Salt and freshly ground pepper

- 1 tablespoon bacon fat *or* vegetable oil
- 1½ cups sliced mushrooms (about 4 ounces)
- 4 tablespoons chopped fresh parsley

- 1 to 1½ cups sour cream, room temperature

For palacsinta: Combine milk, eggs, paprika and salt in medium bowl and whisk to blend. Gradually add flour, whisking until smooth. Blend in melted butter. (Batter can also be made in processor or blender.) Strain batter. Stir in parsley. Refrigerate 1 to 2 hours.

Thin batter with small amount of cold water if necessary *(batter should be consistency of whipping cream)*. Place heavy crepe pan or 5- to 7-inch skillet over medium-high heat. Brush with oil. Add 2 to 2½ tablespoons batter to corner of pan and quickly tilt pan to coat entire bottom. Cook until pancake is lightly browned on bottom. Turn and cook second side until speckled with brown. Slide pancake out of pan onto plate. Repeat with remaining batter, brushing pan with oil as necessary. Stack pancakes (you should have 12 to 16) on plate between sheets of waxed paper. *(Can be prepared up to 3 days ahead, wrapped in plastic and refrigerated. Pancakes can also be frozen. Bring to room temperature before using.)*

For filling and sauce: Heat 3 tablespoons bacon fat or oil in large skillet over medium-high heat. Add chicken, skin side down, and sauté until golden, about 5 minutes. Turn and brown second side. Remove chicken and set aside. Add onions, carrots, bell pepper and celery to skillet and sauté until softened, tossing occasionally, about 6 to 8 minutes. Add garlic and cook 2 minutes. Add paprika and stir 2 minutes; *watch carefully to prevent burning.* Add tomatoes, reduce heat to medium and simmer until slightly thickened, about 3 minutes. Stir in chicken stock and marjoram. Return chicken pieces to skillet skin side up. Bring mixture to boil, then reduce heat, cover and simmer gently until chicken is just opaque and tender, about 15 minutes; *do not overcook.* Remove chicken and set aside.

Strain liquid into medium saucepan, reserving vegetables. Degrease liquid. Puree half of vegetables in blender or processor until smooth. Stir into strained liquid. Season to taste with salt and pepper. Cover and set aside. Transfer remaining vegetables to bowl.

Discard skin and bone from chicken. Cut meat into ½-inch cubes. Add to vegetables. Heat 1 tablespoon bacon fat or oil in large skillet over medium-high heat. Add mushrooms and sauté until liquid evaporates and mushrooms are lightly browned, about 5 minutes. Add to chicken mixture. Add 1 tablespoon parsley and enough sauce to moisten (about 6 tablespoons). Toss gently to combine filling ingredients. Taste and adjust seasoning with salt and freshly ground pepper. *(Sauce and filling can be prepared 6 to 8 hours ahead to this point, covered and kept at room temperature.)*

Preheat oven to 400°F. Grease large gratin or baking dish. Spread several tablespoons of sauce in bottom. Spoon several tablespoons of filling onto second-cooked side of 1 pancake and roll up. Place in dish seam side down. Repeat with remaining pancakes. Cover tightly with aluminum foil. *(Can be assembled up to 3 hours ahead to this point.)* Bake until heated through, about 20 minutes.

Bring sauce to gentle simmer. Blend in enough sour cream to make sauce a deep salmon color, about ⅔ cup. Heat through; *do not boil or mixture will curdle.* Stir in 1 to 2 tablespoons parsley. Taste and adjust seasoning. Spoon sauce in strip along centers of pancakes. Top each with dollop of sour cream and sprinkle with remaining parsley. Serve immediately.

*Hungarian sweet paprika and a pinch of ground red pepper can be substituted.

Chicken in Triple Mustard Sauce

A simple salad of curly endive, french fries and a dry white wine go well with this tangy dish.

4 servings

2 tablespoons (¼ stick) butter
6 chicken breast halves
3 tablespoons butter
1 cup slivered leek, white part only
1 garlic clove, finely minced
½ cup dry white wine
2 tablespoons white wine vinegar
½ cup whipping cream
2 tablespoons Tarragon Mustard (see following recipes)

2 tablespoons Moutarde des Trois Herbes Vertes (see following recipes)
2 tablespoons Dijon mustard
1 tablespoon fresh lemon juice
Salt and freshly ground white pepper

Melt 2 tablespoons butter in heavy large skillet over medium-high heat until foamy. Add chicken breasts and sauté on both sides until golden. Reduce heat to low, cover and simmer 10 minutes. Transfer chicken to platter and keep warm. Discard fat from skillet. Add 3 tablespoons butter to skillet. Stir in leek and cook until limp. Add garlic and stir 1 minute. Increase heat to high, add white wine and wine vinegar and cook until reduced by half. Reduce heat to medium, add cream and mustards and cook, stirring until sauce is thick and bubbly. Blend in lemon juice. Add salt and pepper.

Spoon some sauce into center of each serving plate. Top with chicken. Spoon more sauce over and serve.

Tarragon Mustard

This sauce is also good with cold shellfish and steamed vegetables.

Makes about 4 cups

2 cups dry mustard
1 cup sugar
¾ cup tarragon vinegar
½ cup snipped fresh tarragon *or* 2 tablespoons dried

1 teaspoon salt
½ cup olive oil

Combine all ingredients except olive oil in processor or blender and mix until smooth and creamy. With machine running, add olive oil through feed tube in slow steady stream and blend until mixture is consistency of mayonnaise, stopping frequently to scrape down bowl. Pour into jar with tight-fitting lid. Store in cool, dark place.

Moutarde des Trois Herbes Vertes

Makes about 1½ cups

¼ cup packed parsley sprigs
¼ cup packed fresh tarragon leaves

¼ cup packed fresh dill
1 cup prepared Dijon mustard

Combine parsley sprigs, tarragon and dill in processor and mix until finely chopped (or mince by hand). Add mustard and blend until smooth. Transfer to jar with tight-fitting lid. Store in cool, dark place.

Chicken-wrapped Sausages with Mushroom-Tomato Sauce

6 servings

6 hot *or* mild Italian sausages
6 chicken breast halves, skins left on, boned and flattened
⅓ cup butter
¼ cup white wine
  Salt and freshly ground pepper

2 tablespoons (¼ stick) butter
1 cup uncooked rice
2 cups chicken stock, at boiling point
¼ cup pine nuts (optional)

2 tablespoons (¼ stick) butter

2 medium onions, chopped
2 bunches green onions, sliced (about 2 cups)
2 garlic cloves, minced
1 pound mushrooms, sliced
3 green bell peppers, seeded, deveined and sliced
2 red bell peppers, seeded, deveined and sliced
2 cups tomato puree
½ cup chopped fresh parsley

Bring large pot of water to boil over high heat. Add sausages and boil until cooked through, about 15 minutes. Let cool; remove casings. Carefully wrap 1 chicken piece around each sausage, securing with toothpicks. Melt ⅓ cup butter in large skillet over medium-high heat. Add chicken and brown on all sides. Add wine with salt and pepper to taste. Reduce heat to medium and cook, turning frequently, until chicken is done, about 10 to 15 minutes.

Meanwhile, melt 2 tablespoons butter in medium skillet over medium heat. Add rice and brown lightly. Add chicken stock and pine nuts. Bring to boil over high heat. Reduce heat to low, cover and simmer until tender, 20 minutes.

Melt 2 tablespoons butter in very large skillet over medium heat. Add onions, green onions and garlic and cook until softened, about 5 minutes; *do not brown*. Add mushrooms, bell peppers, tomato puree, parsley and salt and pepper and cook until vegetables are crisp-tender, 10 minutes.

Transfer rice to heated serving platter. Arrange chicken atop rice. Pour sauce over chicken and serve immediately.

Chicken in Oyster Sauce

2 servings

3 tablespoons butter
1 cup sliced mushrooms
2 to 3 shallots, chopped
2 chicken breast halves, skinned, boned and cut into ¼-inch slices
4 fresh *or* canned oysters, chopped (reserve liquor)

½ cup sour cream
¼ teaspoon dried dillweed, or to taste
Salt and freshly ground pepper
Thinly sliced sourdough rounds, toasted

Melt 2 tablespoons butter in large skillet over medium-high heat. Add mushrooms and shallots and sauté until tender, about 8 minutes. Transfer to platter and set aside. Melt remaining 1 tablespoon butter in same skillet. Add chicken and sauté, turning frequently, until just cooked, about 4 minutes. Add to mushrooms and shallots. Pour oyster liquor into skillet, scraping up any browned bits. Cook until reduced by ¼. Add oysters and sour cream and whisk until well blended. Reduce heat to low and simmer 3 to 5 minutes. Stir in dillweed and salt and pepper. Return chicken, shallots and mushrooms to skillet and cook until heated through, about 2 minutes; *do not boil*. Spoon over toasted sourdough rounds and serve.

Jarlsberg Chicken

6 servings

Butter (for baking dish)
6 tablespoons (¾ stick) butter
2 tablespoons oil
6 chicken breast halves, skinned and boned
¾ pound large white mushrooms, washed, patted dry and stemmed
1 large bunch broccoli, stems peeled and trimmed, cut into spears and cooked al dente
Lemon pepper

2 tablespoons all purpose flour
½ cup chicken stock
½ cup dry white wine
1½ cups shredded Jarlsberg *or* Swiss cheese
Salt and freshly ground white pepper
Shredded Jarlsberg (optional)

Lightly butter large baking dish. Melt 2 tablespoons butter with oil in large heavy skillet over low heat. Add chicken and cook until juices run clear when pricked with fork, about 3 to 5 minutes on each side; *do not overcook*. Remove chicken to platter and set aside. Melt 2 more tablespoons butter in skillet. Add mushrooms and cook over medium-high heat until tender, about 3 to 5 minutes. Arrange broccoli in single layer in bottom of dish. Season chicken with lemon pepper. Arrange in single layer over broccoli.

Preheat broiler. Melt remaining 2 tablespoons butter in 1-quart saucepan over low heat. Whisk in flour and cook, stirring constantly, about 3 minutes. Pour in chicken stock and wine, whisking until thoroughly blended. Continue cooking, stirring until sauce thickens and coats spoon. Add 1½ cups cheese and stir until melted. Taste and season with salt and white pepper. Pour sauce over chicken. Arrange mushrooms on top. Sprinkle additional cheese over if desired. Broil about 6 inches from heat source until top is bubbly and golden, about 3 to 5 minutes, watching carefully. Serve immediately.

Chicken Breasts Mediterranean

The sauce is especially flavorful if prepared a day or two before serving. It can be stored up to 2 weeks in the refrigerator or 6 months in the freezer.

6 servings

Sauce

- 3 tablespoons olive oil
- 1 tablespoon butter
- 1 large red onion, minced
- 2 cups drained whole Italian plum tomatoes
- ¼ cup dry Marsala
- 2 garlic cloves, mashed
- ½ teaspoon dried basil
- ½ teaspoon dried oregano
- ¼ teaspoon dried thyme
- ¼ teaspoon finely crumbled bay leaf
- ¼ teaspoon coriander seed
- ¼ teaspoon fennel seed
- 1 piece orange peel
  Salt and freshly ground pepper
  Minced fresh parsley

- 3 tablespoons butter
- 1 tablespoon olive oil
- 6 large chicken breast halves, skinned, boned and flattened to ¼-inch thickness
- 6 tablespoons freshly grated Parmesan cheese
  Minced fresh parsley (garnish)

For sauce: Heat oil with butter in Dutch oven over medium-high heat. Add onion and sauté until golden. Stir in remaining sauce ingredients except parsley and simmer 1 hour. Remove from heat and add minced parsley to taste.

Heat butter with oil in large skillet over medium-high heat. Add chicken and sauté until cooked through, about 3 minutes on each side. Transfer to ovenproof platter and divide sauce among pieces. Sprinkle with Parmesan and run under broiler until sauce bubbles. Garnish with parsley and serve immediately.

❦ Stir-Fried

Chinese Shredded Chicken and Pork with Green Chilies

Perfect served with steamed rice and shredded cucumber tossed in a vinegar and sesame seed oil dressing.

3 to 4 servings

- ¾ pound chicken breasts, skinned, boned and finely shredded
- ½ pound lean pork, finely shredded
- 3 tablespoons cider vinegar
- 1½ tablespoons soy sauce
- 1 teaspoon dry Sherry
- ¼ teaspoon hot chili powder *or* ground red pepper

- ¼ cup cornstarch

- 6 green onions, cut into 1½-inch pieces
- 2 tablespoons shredded fresh mild green chili
- ¼ teaspoon salt
- ¼ teaspoon freshly ground pepper
  Pinch of sugar

- 3 cups vegetable oil
- ½ cup tiny frozen peas, thawed

Combine chicken, pork, vinegar, soy sauce, Sherry and chili powder or red pepper in bowl and marinate 1 hour.

Place cornstarch in shallow bowl. Combine green onions and chili in another bowl. Mix salt, pepper and sugar in separate bowl and set aside.

Heat oil in wok or large skillet to 375°F. Drain meat mixture and toss in cornstarch. Add to wok in small batches, separating shreds with fork. Cook until crisp. Transfer to paper towels to drain. Pour off all but 3 tablespoons oil from wok. Heat remaining oil until hot. Add green onions and chili and stir-fry 30 seconds. Add salt, pepper and sugar, stir-frying for 10 seconds. Add peas and meat and stir-fry just until heated through. Serve immediately.

Kung Pao Chicken

2 servings

2 chicken breast halves, skinned, boned and cubed
1 egg white, lightly beaten
2 teaspoons cornstarch
2 tablespoons black bean sauce*
2 tablespoons water
1 garlic clove, minced
1 tablespoon hoisin sauce*
1 tablespoon rice vinegar

2 teaspoons Sherry
1 teaspoon sugar
2 tablespoons vegetable oil
½ cup raw unsalted peanuts
1 to 2 dried red chilies, crushed, *or* 1 teaspoon dried red pepper flakes
Steamed rice (optional)

Combine chicken, egg white and cornstarch in small bowl. Mix next 7 ingredients in another small bowl. Set sauce aside. Heat oil in wok or heavy large skillet over medium-high heat. Add peanuts and chilies and cook until peanuts are golden brown, about 1 minute. Remove with slotted spoon and set aside. Increase heat to high. Add chicken mixture and stir-fry until chicken is lightly browned, about 1 to 1½ minutes. Reduce heat to medium. Return peanuts to wok. Add sauce and blend thoroughly. Cook until heated through, about 1 to 1½ minutes. Serve immediately over freshly steamed rice if desired.

*Available in oriental markets.

Chicken with Green Peppers

2 servings

2 chicken breast halves, skinned and boned
2 tablespoons dry Sherry
2 tablespoons dark soy sauce
1 tablespoon cornstarch

3 tablespoons peanut oil
1 garlic clove, minced
½ inch fresh ginger, minced
8 large dried black mushrooms, softened in hot water, stems removed, caps quartered
4 branches bok choy (Chinese cabbage), including some of green tops, sliced diagonally

½ green bell pepper, seeded and cut vertically into ⅛-inch strips
2 tomatoes, unpeeled, cored and cut irregularly
Cornstarch

¾ cup chicken stock
1 tablespoon dark soy sauce
2 teaspoons cornstarch
1 teaspoon sesame oil
Cilantro (coriander) sprigs (garnish)
Steamed rice

Remove small fillets from chicken and remove tough tendon. Cut meat into slices ½ inch thick and about 2 inches long. Combine next 3 ingredients, add chicken and marinate 30 minutes.

Heat oil in wok. Add garlic, ginger and chicken and stir-fry until chicken turns white, about 2 minutes. Add mushrooms, bok choy and pepper and stir-fry

1 minute. Sprinkle tomatoes with cornstarch and let stand (*this thickens liquid in tomatoes as they cook*).

Combine next 3 ingredients. Add to wok and stir-fry about 1 minute. Add tomatoes and continue stir-frying until sauce is clear, about 2 minutes. Add sesame oil and toss gently but thoroughly. Spoon into serving dish and garnish with cilantro. Serve with freshly steamed rice.

Szechwan Spicy Tangerine Chicken

Four distinctive Szechwan ingredients—chili paste with garlic, fresh tangerine peel, dried chili peppers and Szechwan peppercorns—make this a rich and complex dish. Serve over fresh Chinese noodles, cellophane noodles or a thin egg noodle such as vermicelli.

2 to 3 servings

1½ pounds boned and skinned chicken breasts, cut into cubes or sliced thin
1 teaspoon cornstarch

⅔ cup diced onion
4 green onions, cut into 1-inch lengths or smaller
5 dried chili peppers, minced
2 teaspoons Szechwan peppercorns,* roasted and ground
2 teaspoons minced fresh ginger
2 tablespoons fresh tangerine juice or orange juice

2 tablespoons dark soy sauce
1 tablespoon hoisin sauce*
¾ teaspoon sugar
¾ teaspoon Szechwan chili paste with garlic*

2 cups oil

2 tablespoons tangerine peel or orange peel cut into strips
1 teaspoon vinegar
1 teaspoon sesame oil*

Combine chicken and cornstarch. Set aside.

Combine onions in small bowl. Combine chili peppers, peppercorns and ginger in another bowl. Combine juice, soy sauce, hoisin, sugar and chili paste and mix well. Set all 3 bowls aside.

Heat oil in wok to 225°F. Add chicken and cook until it loses pink color. Remove chicken and drain. Pour out all but 1 tablespoon of oil.

Heat oil until very hot. Add chili pepper mixture and stir-fry 15 seconds. Add peel. Add combined onions and stir-fry 20 seconds. Mix in chicken. Add juice mixture and stir-fry 30 seconds. Add vinegar and stir-fry 15 seconds. Mix in sesame oil and serve.

*Available in oriental markets.

Chicken Dijon Penne

6 to 8 servings

3 whole chicken breasts, skinned, boned and cut into 1-inch cubes
Salt and freshly ground pepper
¼ cup (½ stick) butter
2 cups whipping cream
1 tablespoon olive oil
Salt

1 pound medium penne pasta
½ cup Dijon mustard
3 tablespoons finely chopped fresh parsley
2 tablespoons minced fresh chives

Season chicken with salt and pepper. Melt butter in large skillet over medium-high heat until bubbly. Add chicken and stir-fry until tender, about 3 minutes.

Remove from skillet and set aside. Add cream to skillet, stirring to blend well. Bring mixture to boil. Reduce heat and simmer until mixture is reduced and slightly thickened, about 5 minutes. Meanwhile, bring large amount of water to boil with olive oil and salt. Add pasta and cook until al dente. Drain well. Transfer to heated serving dish. Whisk mustard into cream mixture. Return chicken to skillet, reduce heat to low and cook until heated through; *do not boil*. Spoon chicken mixture over pasta. Add parsley and chives and toss thoroughly.

🍂 Fried

Southern Fried Chicken

2 servings

2 small chicken legs
2 small chicken thighs
2 small chicken breast halves
1 cup buttermilk

½ cup all purpose flour
1 teaspoon salt
½ teaspoon ground sage

¼ teaspoon paprika
¼ teaspoon freshly ground pepper
2 eggs, lightly beaten with 1 tablespoon water
1 cup fine dry breadcrumbs

Oil (for deep frying)

Rinse chicken pieces; pat dry with paper towels. Arrange in shallow dish. Pour buttermilk over chicken, coating evenly. Marinate at room temperature 30 minutes, turning occasionally.

Combine flour, salt, sage, paprika and pepper in paper bag. Add chicken to bag in batches and shake to cover with flour mixture. Dip chicken into egg mixture, then roll in breadcrumbs. Let stand on rack 15 minutes.

Pour oil into 10-inch skillet or electric frypan to depth of 1 inch and heat to 375°F. Add chicken legs and thighs and fry, turning frequently with tongs, until browned, about 12 minutes. Fry breasts about 8 minutes. As chicken pieces are cooked, transfer to paper towels and drain. Serve hot or at room temperature.

Batter-Dipped Chicken

Try this as an hors d'oeuvre or as a light dinner with stir-fried vegetables.

6 servings

Oil (for deep frying)
1 cup instant pancake mix
¾ cup milk
Garlic powder
Salt and freshly ground pepper

3 whole chicken breasts, skinned, boned and cut into 1-inch cubes
Hot mustard *or* sweet and sour sauce

Heat oil in deep fryer to 370°F. Combine pancake mix and milk in shallow dish. Season with garlic powder and salt and pepper. Dip chicken pieces in batter, coating well. Fry in batches until golden, about 1 minute. Drain on paper towels. Serve with hot mustard or sweet and sour sauce.

Double-fried Chicken with Ginger and Sesame Oil (Kara-age)

6 servings

1 2½- to 3-pound chicken
¼ cup Japanese soy sauce
¼ cup saké *or* dry Sherry
1 1-inch piece fresh ginger, minced
1 garlic clove, minced

½ cup all purpose flour
½ cup cornstarch

Salt
Kona sansho (Japanese fragrant pepper)* *or* freshly ground pepper

Oil (for deep frying)
Sesame oil*
Lemon wedges (garnish)

Cut chicken into 12 pieces, quartering breast and halving thighs crosswise. Combine soy sauce, saké, ginger and garlic in shallow baking dish. Add chicken, turning to coat all sides. Let chicken marinate at room temperature 30 minutes, turning frequently.

Combine flour, cornstarch, salt and kona sansho or pepper in shallow bowl. Dredge chicken in flour mixture, shaking off excess. Transfer chicken to waxed paper. Let stand until chicken is not completely white, 10 minutes.

Heat oil in wok or deep fryer to 360°F, adding a few drops of sesame oil. Add chicken to oil in batches and fry just until lightly colored, about 45 seconds to 1 minute. Drain well on paper towels. Reduce oil temperature to 325°F. Return chicken to oil in batches and fry until coating is brown and chicken is cooked through, about 6 to 10 minutes. Drain on paper towels. Serve at room temperature with lemon wedges.

*Available in oriental markets.

Vegetable-filled Chicken Breast Rolls

6 servings

Tomato Dipping Sauce
2½ pounds tomatoes, quartered (about 6 large)
2 ¼-inch-thick slices fresh ginger (from root about ½ inch in diameter)
½ teaspoon salt
¼ teaspoon sesame oil

1 large carrot, cut into 2½ × ¼-inch julienne slices

12 green beans, trimmed and cut into 2½-inch lengths

6 chicken breast halves, boned and skinned
Salt
1 tablespoon dried sage
½ cup all purpose flour
½ cup cornstarch

Vegetable oil (for deep frying)

For sauce: Combine tomatoes and ginger in large saucepan over low heat. Cover and cook, stirring and mashing with back of spoon, until tomatoes are very soft and liquid is almost completely evaporated, about 40 minutes. Remove ginger and set aside. Puree tomatoes in food mill or sieve, pressing with back of spoon to extract all pulp. Return to saucepan. Add ginger and simmer gently over low heat until thickened and reduced to about 1⅓ cups. Blend in salt and sesame oil. Adjust seasoning. Discard ginger pieces. Let cool to room temperature.

Blanch carrot and green beans in boiling salted water, about 1 minute. Plunge into cold water to stop cooking process. Drain and set aside.

Lightly coat 2 sheets of waxed paper with melted butter or oil. Place chicken breast halves between oiled sides of paper and pound gently until almost transparent (about 1/16 inch thick). Season with salt. Roll 2 beans and 1 carrot stick in each chicken breast half; secure with unwaxed dental floss or string. Place water in steamer or in large saucepan to 1 inch from rack. Add sage to water. Place over high heat and bring to boil. Meanwhile, mix flour and cornstarch on large plate. Arrange rolls on steamer rack, spacing evenly. Cover and steam 1 minute. Discard string or floss. Immediately dredge rolls in flour mixture. Cool to room temperature.

Pour oil into heavy-bottomed large skillet to depth of 2 inches and heat to 360°F. Add chicken (in batches if necessary; *do not crowd*) and fry until lightly browned on all sides, 2 to 3 minutes. Remove with slotted spoon and drain on paper towels. Cut each roll into ½-inch-thick slices. Serve immediately and pass sauce separately.

Stuffed Deep-fried Chicken Wings (Peek Gai Yod Sai)

Boning chicken wings may take some time and patience at first, but it becomes progressively easier. Always use your sharpest knife for best results.

6 servings

6 chicken wings

1 cooked Chinese sausage,* skinned and coarsely chopped (about ⅓ cup)

1 tablespoon chopped fresh cilantro (coriander)

1 tablespoon fish sauce (nam pla)*

1 teaspoon salt

1 tablespoon freshly ground pepper

2 garlic cloves, chopped

6 canned water chestnuts, drained and finely chopped

4 dried oriental mushrooms, soaked in hot water until soft, hard cores discarded and caps finely chopped

4 green onions, chopped (⅔ to ¾ cup)

2 ounces uncooked long-grain rice *or* bean threads (cellophane noodles),* soaked in hot water 3 to 4 minutes, drained and chopped (about 1 generous cup)

1 medium carrot, grated (⅔ to ¾ cup)

4 cups vegetable oil (for deep frying)

¼ cup rice flour

1 egg, beaten
Chili Sauce with Tamarind (see following recipe)

To bone chicken wings, bend both wing joints of 1 wing in opposite directions to loosen bones and tendons. Using very sharp knife, cut ring around top of largest bone (one that separates from body of bird). Using thumbs, pry and separate skin and meat down first bone to joint, scraping with knife tip where meat adheres to bone, turning back skin over unboned part as you proceed. When first bone is entirely exposed, break it off from 2 smaller bones below. Place the knife point under skin and gently move it completely around the joint, detaching skin from underlying flesh and bone. Continue to scrape and roll back skin from 2 smaller bones. Peel flesh back from exposed ends of 2 smaller bones and cut them apart from each other at top. Peel skin down bones until you reach lower end near wing tip. Break bones off (smaller bone is easier) from remaining cartilage and skin that make up wing tip and carefully turn entire skin right side out, checking for bone splinters, holes and punctures. Repeat with remaining wings. Set skins aside. Measure 1 cup chicken meat.

Chop reserved 1 cup chicken meat. Transfer to processor or blender. Add sausage, cilantro, fish sauce, salt and pepper and garlic and mix to finely textured paste. Transfer to medium bowl. Add water chestnuts, mushrooms, onions, rice and carrot and blend thoroughly. Fill reserved skins with stuffing, using thumb to tamp stuffing down to bottom and distribute evenly. Seal top flaps of skin over one another.

Heat oil in wok to 375°F. Pour rice flour onto large plate. Roll each wing in flour, dusting off excess. Holding 1 wing at tip, dip into beaten egg and drop gently into heated oil. Repeat with another wing. Fry both wings until crisp and golden brown, about 5 minutes per side. Remove from oil using slotted spoon and drain on paper towels. Return oil to 375°F. Repeat with remaining wings 2 at a time. Serve hot. Pass sauce separately.

*Available in oriental markets.

Chili Sauce with Tamarind (Nam Prik Som Mak Kam)

Makes about ½ cup

1 tablespoon dried shrimp powder*
4 small dried red chilies, seeded and minced
4 medium garlic cloves, minced
1 teaspoon shrimp paste (kapee)* *or* 1 teaspoon anchovy paste

¼ cup fish sauce (nam pla)*
1 tablespoon plus 1½ teaspoons palm sugar *or* dark brown sugar
1 tablespoon tamarind pulp concentrate* dissolved in 3 tablespoons hot water

Blend shrimp powder, chilies and garlic in small bowl. Mix in shrimp paste. Add fish sauce, sugar and tamarind and stir until sugar is dissolved. Pour into small bowl and serve.

*Available in oriental markets.

Chicken with Walnuts in Plum Sauce

4 servings

Water, at boiling point
1 cup walnut halves

1 tablespoon beaten egg
1 tablespoon oil
1 teaspoon cornstarch
6 chicken thighs (about 1½ pounds), boned, skinned and cut into ½-inch pieces

½ cup oil

2 tablespoons plum sauce* *or* hoisin sauce*
1 1-inch piece fresh ginger, peeled and finely chopped
1 teaspoon sugar
1 teaspoon soy sauce
¼ teaspoon sesame oil*
2 green onions, finely chopped (garnish)

Pour boiling water over walnuts and let stand 5 minutes. Drain and pat dry.

Combine egg with 1 tablespoon oil and cornstarch in small bowl. Add chicken pieces and toss gently to coat evenly.

Heat ½ cup oil in wok over medium-high heat until haze forms. Add walnuts and fry until golden, about 45 seconds. Remove with slotted spoon and drain on paper towels. Add chicken to wok and cook until golden, about 3 minutes. Drain.

Pour off all but thin film of oil. Return pan to heat, add plum or hoisin sauce, ginger, sugar, soy sauce and sesame oil and stir until combined. Reduce heat and simmer, stirring constantly, until sauce begins to glisten, about 1 to 2 minutes. Add chicken and walnuts and mix thoroughly with sauce. Transfer to heated serving platter and garnish with green onions.

*Available in oriental markets.

❧ Salads and Sandwiches

Chicken-Walnut Salad

2 servings

2 tablespoons (¼ stick) butter
1 tablespoon oil
1 whole chicken breast, boned, skinned and pounded lightly
1 teaspoon fresh lemon juice
Salt and freshly ground pepper

Dressing
6 tablespoons olive oil
3 tablespoons cider vinegar
½ teaspoon dry mustard
Salt and freshly ground pepper

Salad
2 celery stalks, cut into julienne slices

¼ head romaine, cut into thin crosswise strips
2 ounces Gruyère cheese, cut into julienne slices
¼ cup coarsely chopped walnuts

10 walnut halves, toasted
Pimiento strips (garnish)
Minced fresh parsley (garnishes)

Melt butter with oil in small skillet over medium-low heat. Add chicken, turning to coat all sides. Sprinkle with lemon juice and salt and pepper. Cover with circle of waxed paper and skillet lid. Poach until chicken is cooked through, about 12 minutes. Remove from heat and let cool, covered, in pan.

For dressing: Combine all ingredients in small bowl and whisk to blend well.
For salad: Toss salad ingredients. Add half of dressing and toss again.

Cut chicken breast halves, then cut each half crosswise into 5 slices. Transfer to small bowl. Moisten with some of poaching liquid and toss gently with remaining dressing. Divide lettuce mixture among plates. Arrange chicken slices over top, placing a walnut half on each slice. Crisscross with pimiento strips and sprinkle with minced parsley.

Chicken and Melon Salad with Green Chili Mayonnaise

A cool and attractive luncheon dish.

4 to 6 servings

2 tablespoons (¼ stick) butter
2 whole chicken breasts, boned, skinned, and slightly flattened to even thickness

½ honeydew melon, peeled, seeded and sliced, room temperature

Green Chili Mayonnaise (see following recipe)
Lime slices (garnish)
Parsley sprigs (garnish)

Preheat oven to 350°F. Cut piece of waxed paper or foil to fit heavy skillet large enough to hold chicken in 1 layer. Set paper aside. Melt butter in skillet. Add chicken to melted butter, turning just until surface of meat begins to whiten. Press waxed paper or foil over chicken. Cover skillet tightly with lid and bake just until juices run clear, about 8 minutes; do not overcook. Drain chicken.

Slice chicken. Alternate chicken and melon in fan pattern on platter or individual plates. Cover and refrigerate. Let stand at room temperature 15 to 20 minutes before serving. Spoon Green Chili Mayonnaise across top. Garnish with lime and parsley and serve.

Green Chili Mayonnaise

This is also terrific with fish or beef and makes a flavorful sandwich spread.

Makes about 1½ cups

2 egg yolks, room temperature
1 tablespoon fresh lime juice
1 tablespoon chopped onion
1½ cups oil

½ teaspoon salt
    Pinch of freshly ground pepper
2 tablespoons chopped green chili

Mix yolks and lime juice in processor or blender. Blend in onion. With machine running, add oil in slow, steady stream, processing until mayonnaise is smooth and thick. Mix in salt and pepper. Transfer to bowl and stir in green chili.

Sesame Chicken Salad

4 servings

2 poached whole chicken breasts
    (about 2 pounds meat), skinned
    and cut into ¼-inch strips
½ pound snow peas, halved and
    blanched
7 water chestnuts, sliced
4 whole green onions, sliced
    diagonally
½ cup sesame seed, lightly toasted
    Salt and freshly ground pepper

2 tablespoons dry Sherry
1 egg yolk

1½ tablespoons fresh lemon juice
1 tablespoon Dijon mustard
1 tablespoon soy sauce (preferably
    dark)
1 teaspoon sugar
½ teaspoon minced fresh ginger *or*
    ¼ teaspoon ground
¼ cup olive oil
¼ cup safflower oil *or* peanut oil
    Hot pepper sauce *or* dried red
    pepper flakes

Combine chicken, snow peas, water chestnuts, onions, sesame seed and salt and pepper in bowl and toss lightly.

Mix Sherry, egg yolk, lemon juice, mustard, soy sauce, sugar and ginger in processor or small bowl and blend well. Gradually add oils, beating constantly until mixture is emulsified. Add hot pepper sauce or pepper flakes to taste. Pour over chicken and toss well. Serve chilled or at room temperature.

Chicken Pasta Salad with Fruit

4 servings

3 whole chicken breasts, boned,
    cooked and chopped into bite-size
    pieces
2 cups seedless green grapes
1 cup snow peas
12 spinach leaves, torn into pieces
1 large celery heart with leaves,
    chopped
7 ounces 1-inch cheese raviolini,*
    cooked, drained and cooled
1 6-ounce jar artichoke hearts with
    marinade
1 kiwi, peeled and sliced

½ large cucumber, sliced
½ cup raisins
1 green onion, chopped
⅔ cup mayonnaise
½ cup freshly grated Parmesan
    cheese
⅓ cup fresh lemon juice
    Salt and freshly ground white
    pepper
    Spinach leaves
    Mandarin orange sections
    (garnish)

Combine first 11 ingredients in large serving bowl and toss gently. Mix mayonnaise, Parmesan cheese, lemon juice and salt and white pepper in small bowl. Pour over salad and toss again. Refrigerate until ready to use. To serve, spoon salad onto spinach-lined plates. Garnish with mandarin orange sections.

*Available in Italian markets.

Smoked Chicken, Apple and Walnut Salad

Accompany with a crisp Chenin Blanc. Smoked turkey breast can be substituted.

6 servings

4 smoked whole chicken breasts (about 2 pounds), skinned and cut into thin strips
3 medium Granny Smith apples *or* other tart apples, cored and diced
6 celery stalks, sliced (1½ cups)
4 cups loosely packed chopped watercress leaves

1 cup Lemon-Mustard Dressing (see following recipe)
Freshly ground pepper

Boston *or* romaine lettuce leaves
Watercress sprigs (garnish)
1¼ cups chopped walnuts, toasted (5 ounces)

Toss chicken strips, apples, celery and chopped watercress in large bowl. Blend in lemon dressing and pepper. Cover and refrigerate up to 4 hours.

To serve, line platter with lettuce. Mound salad in center. Garnish with watercress sprigs. Sprinkle with nuts.

Lemon-Mustard Dressing

Makes 1 cup

4 teaspoons fresh lemon juice
4 teaspoons Dijon mustard
1 egg yolk
¼ teaspoon *each* salt and freshly ground pepper

1 cup olive oil
1 tablespoon fresh lemon juice

Combine 4 teaspoons lemon juice with mustard, yolk, salt and pepper in processor or blender. With machine running, add olive oil in slow, steady stream and mix until thickened. Blend in remaining lemon juice.

Molded Chicken Salad (Bouquet de Poulet)

This is perfect for a picnic lunch.

4 to 6 servings

4 cups chicken stock (preferably homemade)
2 large chicken breast halves

1 large head cauliflower, cut into florets (stems peeled, reserved and diced)
3 small crookneck squash, thinly sliced lengthwise, neck part diced
1 large bunch broccoli, cut into florets (stems peeled, reserved and diced)
Salt and freshly ground pepper

Broccoli Mayonnaise
2 egg yolks, room temperature
1 tablespoon red wine vinegar

1 teaspoon Dijon mustard
¾ cup peanut oil
¼ cup walnut oil
2 tablespoons fresh lemon juice
1 tablespoon minced fresh tarragon *or* 1 teaspoon dried
Salt and freshly ground pepper
Pinch of ground red pepper

3 tablespoons chopped walnuts, toasted
Parsley, watercress *or* crisp greens (garnish)
1 teaspoon minced fresh chives

Bring stock to simmer in large saucepan over low heat. Add chicken breast and reduce heat so stock is barely simmering. Cover and poach until chicken is springy to the touch, about 8 minutes. Remove chicken using slotted spoon.

Add enough water to stock to cover vegetables. Bring to boil. Add cauliflower florets and cook until tender when pierced with knife, about 3 to 5 minutes. Remove with slotted spoon and plunge into ice water to stop cooking process. Drain and set aside. Repeat with cauliflower stems, cooking 3 to 5 minutes, and diced squash, cooking 1 minute. Set aside in separate bowl. Repeat for squash slices, cooking 1 minute. Add to cauliflower florets. Repeat with broccoli florets, cooking 3 minutes. Add to cauliflower florets. Repeat for broccoli stems, cooking 3 minutes. Drain and add to cauliflower stems and diced squash. Sprinkle with salt and freshly ground pepper.

Line 3-quart round-bottomed bowl with aluminum foil, allowing several inches overhang. Cut large broccoli and cauliflower florets in half crosswise. Arrange largest florets stems up in center of bowl. Arrange remaining florets (stems up) with sides touching until bottom is filled, then work up sides. Overlap slices of squash around sides of bowl above broccoli and cauliflower.

For mayonnaise: Combine yolks, vinegar and mustard in medium bowl and beat until thick and lemon colored. Whisk in peanut oil 1 drop at a time until well blended. Whisk in walnut oil 1 drop at a time. Add lemon juice, tarragon, salt and peppers and mix well.

Skin, bone and coarsely dice chicken. Combine chicken, broccoli stems, cauliflower stems, diced squash and walnuts in another medium bowl. Add ¾ of mayonnaise and mix well. Carefully spoon mixture over broccoli and cauliflower florets, spreading so that it does not extend above top of squash layer. *(Can be made ahead to this point and refrigerated. Bring to room temperature before serving.)* Unmold onto platter and gently remove foil. Garnish with watercress or crisp greens. Just before serving, mix chives with remaining mayonnaise to pass with salad.

Chicken Salad with Wild Rice

4 servings

½ cup uncooked wild rice
1½ cups water
   Salt
 2 cups diced poached chicken
 1 cup watercress leaves
½ cup thinly sliced green onion
½ cup diced celery
½ cup blanched almonds, chopped
   and toasted

Tarragon Vinaigrette
½ cup olive oil
¼ cup white wine vinegar
 1 tablespoon chopped fresh
   tarragon *or* 1 teaspoon dried
 1 teaspoon coarse salt
½ teaspoon freshly ground pepper

Rinse rice under running water. Bring 1½ cups salted water to rapid boil in medium saucepan over high heat. Stir in rice and return water to rapid boil. Stir rice with fork and reduce heat so water simmers gently. Cover and cook until grains puff open and white interior of rice appears, about 25 to 35 minutes. Rinse rice under cold water; drain well. Transfer to large bowl. Add chicken, watercress, green onion, diced celery and chopped almonds.

For vinaigrette: Whisk oil into vinegar in medium bowl 1 drop at a time. Stir in tarragon, salt and pepper. Pour small amount of vinaigrette over chicken salad and toss gently, adding more vinaigrette a little at a time until evenly coated. Serve slightly chilled.

Stir-fried Chicken Salad with Szechwan Noodles

6 servings

3 chicken breast halves, skinned, boned and cut into ³⁄₈-inch julienne slices

3 tablespoons vegetable oil

Salt

1¼ pounds fresh *or* dried Chinese egg noodles

1 tablespoon vegetable oil

3 large red bell peppers

5 green onions, cut diagonally into ¼-inch pieces

3 tablespoons white wine vinegar

2½ to 3 tablespoons chili oil*

2½ to 3 tablespoons sesame oil*

2 teaspoons sugar

2 teaspoons salt

1½ teaspoons Szechwan peppercorns,* ground in mortar and strained

¾ teaspoon freshly ground pepper

6 tablespoons vegetable oil

Pat chicken dry. Heat 3 tablespoons vegetable oil in wok or heavy large skillet over medium-high heat until very hot but not smoking. Add chicken and stir-fry just until opaque, about 3 minutes. Set chicken aside.

Bring large amount of salted water to rapid boil over high heat. Add noodles and cook until firm but tender to the bite (al dente). Drain well. Transfer to large bowl. Add 1 tablespoon vegetable oil and toss gently to coat.

Broil peppers 6 inches from heat source, turning occasionally, until all sides are blackened. Transfer peppers to plastic bag and seal tightly. Set aside 10 minutes to steam. Slip charred skins off peppers and discard. Cut out stem and seeds. Rinse peppers if necessary to remove any seeds; pat dry. Cut into ¼-inch julienne.

Combine onions, vinegar, hot chili oil, sesame oil, sugar, salt, Szechwan peppercorns and freshly ground pepper in medium bowl. Heat remaining 6 tablespoons vegetable oil in small saucepan until very hot but not smoking. Pour hot oil over onion mixture in thin steady stream, stirring constantly. Set aside for 15 minutes *(hot oil will release flavor of spices)*.

Reserve some of red bell pepper for garnish; add remaining red pepper to noodles. Add green onion mixture and chicken and toss gently using fork or chopsticks. Arrange reserved red pepper strips over top. Cover with plastic wrap and refrigerate. Bring to room temperature. Adjust seasoning and serve.

* Available in oriental markets.

Chicken and Chili Buns

Sliced tomatoes spread with guacamole are great on a picnic with these spicy buns. For dessert, you could serve spiked melon wedges: Cut a plug from a honeydew or watermelon the night before the picnic. Pour in a little rum and refit the plug (seal it with tape). Let melon stand overnight. The rum will have soaked into the melon by serving time.

Makes 10 buns

Dough
- 1 cup water, at boiling point
- ½ cup cornmeal
- 1 teaspoon salt
- 2 envelopes dry yeast
- 1 tablespoon sugar
- ½ cup lukewarm water (90°F to 105°F)
- 1 cup milk, warmed slightly
- 2 teaspoons salt
- 4 to 4½ cups all purpose flour

Filling
- ¼ cup olive oil
- ½ cup minced onion
- ¼ cup minced green bell pepper
- 2 tomatoes, peeled, seeded and chopped
- ¼ cup chopped green chili
- 1 to 2 large garlic cloves, minced
- 1 teaspoon dried marjoram
- 1 cup chopped cooked chicken
- 1 cup drained cooked corn
- ½ cup grated Monterey Jack cheese
- 2 tablespoons sour cream
- Salt and freshly ground pepper

- 1 egg beaten with 1 tablespoon whipping cream

For dough: Combine water, cornmeal and salt in small saucepan and cook over medium heat, stirring constantly until thickened, about 4 minutes. Let cool, then transfer to large mixing bowl.

Dissolve yeast and sugar in lukewarm water and let stand until foamy and proofed, 5 to 10 minutes. Blend into cornmeal mixture. Stir in milk and salt. Gradually add flour, stopping when dough pulls away from sides of bowl.

Turn onto lightly floured board and knead until smooth and elastic, about 10 minutes, adding flour as necessary. Place in greased bowl, turning to coat entire surface. Cover and let rise in warm, draft-free area until doubled in size.

For filling: Heat oil in large skillet over medium heat. Add onion and sauté about 5 minutes. Add pepper and sauté another 2 minutes. Blend in tomatoes, chili, garlic and marjoram. Cover and cook 2 minutes longer. Remove lid, increase heat to medium high and continue cooking until liquid has evaporated, about 5 minutes. Transfer to bowl and let cool. Stir in remaining ingredients except beaten egg and whipping cream.

When dough has risen, punch down and knead briefly. Divide in half. Roll one half into 8 × 20-inch rectangle and cut into ten 4-inch squares. Divide chicken mixture among squares, leaving ½-inch border. Roll remaining dough into slightly larger rectangle and then cut into 10 squares. Brush edges of filled squares with egg mixture. Top with unfilled square, sealing edges with tines of fork. Place on baking sheet and let rise about 40 minutes.

About 15 minutes before baking, position rack in upper third of oven and preheat to 375°F. Brush pastries again with egg mixture and bake until golden brown, about 25 to 30 minutes.

Chicken Burgers

Serve chicken burgers on buns with mayonnaise, lettuce and sliced tomatoes. Chopped sautéed mushrooms can also be added to chicken mixture.

6 servings

- 2 cups chopped cooked chicken
- ¼ cup seasoned breadcrumbs
- ¼ cup minced onion
- 2 eggs
- Salt and freshly ground pepper
- 2 to 3 tablespoons oil

Combine chicken, breadcrumbs, onion and eggs in medium bowl and blend well. Season with salt and pepper. Cover and refrigerate until ready to use.

Form chicken mixture into 6 patties. Heat oil in skillet over medium-high heat. Add patties and fry until browned, turning once.

Mexican Tortilla Sandwich

1 serving

Butter
2 8-inch flour tortillas
2 ounces sharp cheddar cheese, shredded

2 ounces cooked chicken, shredded
2 tablespoons chopped red onion
¼ avocado, thinly sliced
2 tablespoons chile salsa

Butter 1 side of each tortilla. Arrange 1 tortilla, buttered side down, in skillet or on cold griddle. Layer cheese, chicken, onion and avocado over, leaving ¼-inch border on all sides. Drizzle evenly with salsa. Top with remaining tortilla, buttered side up. Cook over medium heat, turning once, until tortillas are golden, about 3 to 4 minutes per side.

🍎 Livers

Brioche Filled with Chicken Liver Pâté

The brioche should be begun at least two days before serving to allow for the long risings and later chilling. You can get an even longer head start if you make it ahead and freeze.

6 servings

1½ teaspoons dry yeast
1½ teaspoons sugar
¼ cup lukewarm water (90°F to 105°F)
2 cups all purpose flour
½ cup (1 stick) butter, melted and cooled
1 teaspoon salt

3 eggs, lightly beaten, room temperature

1 egg
1 tablespoon water

Chicken Liver Pâté (see following recipe)

Dissolve yeast and sugar in water in small bowl and let stand until foamy and proofed, 5 to 10 minutes. Using fingertips, mix in ½ cup flour to make smooth ball. Cover and let sponge stand at room temperature until doubled in size.

Combine remaining flour, melted butter, salt and 3 eggs in mixing bowl and beat 2 minutes. Add the sponge and continue beating until smooth. Cover with towel and let rise at room temperature for about 6 hours.

Punch dough down and beat 3 minutes. Cover with plastic; chill at least 12 hours or up to 24 hours.

Butter 5- to 6-cup fluted mold or round baking dish. Form ¾ of dough into smooth ball by kneading lightly and shaping with palms of hands. Place ball in prepared mold. Using fingers, make hole about 2 inches deep in center of ball and spread until about 2 to 3 inches wide. Roll remaining dough between palms to make smaller ball, then pull on one side to make teardrop shape. Insert narrower end into hole in larger ball of dough. Cover and let rise until dough is doubled in size and feels soft and springy to the touch.

Preheat oven to 350°F. Beat egg and water and brush over top of brioche. Bake until glossy and golden brown and brioche has shrunk slightly from sides of mold, about 50 minutes. Immediately remove from mold and let stand on wire rack until completely cooled.

Cut round from bottom of brioche and reserve. Scoop out center crumbs, leaving shell about 1 inch thick. Fill with pâté. Replace reserved round, securing with butter. Wrap and chill thoroughly. Cut into wedges to serve.

Chicken Liver Pâté

½ pound chicken livers	⅛ teaspoon anchovy paste
½ cup (1 stick) butter, cut into pieces, room temperature	Pinch of freshly grated nutmeg
	Pinch of ground cloves
2 tablespoons minced onion	Pinch of ground red pepper
¾ teaspoon dry mustard	Salt

Cover livers with water in small saucepan. Bring to boil, then reduce heat and simmer until tender, about 20 minutes. Remove from heat and let cool completely in liquid. Drain well.

Transfer livers to processor or blender. Add butter and mix until smooth and fluffy. Mix in remaining ingredients. Taste and adjust seasoning. Chill completely before packing into brioche.

Mushroom–Chicken Liver Sauté

2 to 4 servings

5 tablespoons butter	½ teaspoon freshly ground pepper
1 pound chicken livers, patted dry	⅛ teaspoon dried oregano
1 large onion, sliced	⅛ teaspoon hot pepper sauce
½ pound mushrooms, sliced	2 tablespoons sweet vermouth
2 tablespoons wine vinegar	Freshly cooked rice *or* cooked
1 teaspoon Worcestershire sauce	noodles
1 teaspoon salt	

Melt 3 tablespoons butter in large skillet over medium-high heat. Add chicken livers and sauté until browned outside but still pink inside, about 2 to 3 minutes. Remove from skillet with slotted spoon and set aside. Melt 2 more tablespoons butter in same skillet over medium heat. Add onion and mushrooms and sauté until mushrooms are tender, about 5 minutes. Stir in vinegar, Worcestershire sauce, salt, pepper, oregano and hot pepper sauce and cook 5 minutes. Add vermouth and chicken livers and cook until heated through, about 2 minutes. Serve hot over freshly cooked rice or noodles.

Chicken Livers with Ginger and Sherry

4 servings

¼ cup soy sauce	1 large onion, thinly sliced
2 tablespoons dry Sherry	
1 teaspoon brown sugar	All purpose flour
1 teaspoon grated fresh ginger *or* ½ teaspoon ground ginger	Salt and freshly ground pepper
	1 pound chicken livers, trimmed
3 tablespoons butter	

Preheat oven to 200°F. Combine first 4 ingredients in small bowl. Melt 2 tablespoons butter in large skillet over medium-high heat. Add onion and sauté until browned and crisp, about 20 minutes. Transfer to platter and keep warm in oven.

Combine flour and salt and pepper in shallow dish. Dredge livers in flour, shaking off excess. Melt remaining butter in same skillet over medium-high heat. Add livers and brown about 1 minute. Turn livers over and add soy sauce mixture. Continue cooking, basting frequently, until livers are done, about 2 minutes. Arrange over onion and pour pan juices over.

2 ❦ Turkey

Back in the early days of the Republic, when the bald eagle was proposed as the national bird, Benjamin Franklin voiced a strong objection. Why choose the eagle, he argued, when we have the turkey? After all, he said, the turkey is much better looking—even magnificent in its mating plumage. It is very clever, more than a match for most woodsmen. Furthermore, it is our biggest bird, and therefore a fitting symbol for a country whose growth is unlimited. And above all, said Ben, turkey makes for some extraordinarily good eating.

Franklin was overruled, however, and so the eagle is on the twenty-five cent piece. But the turkey is on the Thanksgiving table. And while a quarter doesn't buy much these days, a turkey goes a long way indeed, especially for a creative cook armed with imaginative recipes.

Turkey is, of course, the quintessential holiday bird. But as the recipes in this chapter prove, it need not be reserved just for Thanksgiving, Christmas and a few other special celebrations. Nor is there any rule that says turkey must be served whole. Now that turkey breasts, legs, wings and thighs can be purchased separately all year round, cooks have many more possibilities than they did a decade or so ago. Turkey breast, for example, is skillet-roasted and flavored with shallot and Port in Turkey à l'Orange (page 58), a recipe inspired by the great chef Michel Guérard. Stuffed with a sausage-onion-mushroom mixture, one turkey thigh (page 59) becomes a perfect entrée for two. And to answer the constant question of what to do with leftover turkey, there is a special salad enlivened with almonds and ginger (page 66), cheese and tarragon flavored Turkey Elegant (page 63), and cubed turkey that is curried and served *en brioche* (page 66).

International favorites such as Turkey Mole (page 64) and Turkey Valdostana (page 62) are here, too. And the whole-roasted holiday bird is not neglected: One version features a unique apple-sausage stuffing (page 57; for more stuffings, turn to Chapter Five); another is roasted upside-down, dressed with a cheese-enriched Venetian stuffing and served with rich giblet gravy flavored with Madeira (page 56). In American kitchens and dining rooms, at least, turkey *is* the national bird.

Ben Franklin would be proud.

Upside-Down Roast Turkey

This topsy-turvy turkey is roasted breast down until the last hour or so, when it is turned over to promote even browning and juicy white meat.

If you are using a frozen turkey, thaw it for several days in the refrigerator rather than at room temperature, which creates an incubator effect for harmful bacteria. A frozen turkey can also be thawed in cold water about 12 hours; change the water several times to ensure that it remains cold.

Stuff the turkey just before it goes into the oven, never before. Remove all stuffing from the cavity before refrigerating any leftover turkey.

This turkey would also be marvelous with Herman's Corn Bread Stuffing (see recipe, page 97).

Serves 8 to 10

1 15- to 20-pound turkey (reserve giblets and neck for Giblet Gravy with Wine)
½ to 1 cup chicken stock
  Butter
  Venetian Stuffing with Cheese (see following recipes)
1 garlic clove, minced
1 teaspoon dried basil
1 teaspoon salt

½ teaspoon freshly ground pepper
¼ teaspoon dried rosemary
¼ teaspoon dried marjoram
⅛ teaspoon dried thyme
¾ cup (1½ sticks) unsalted butter, room temperature
1½ cups dry white wine, room temperature
  Giblet Gravy with Wine (see following recipes)

Rinse turkey under cold running water and pat dry with paper towels. *(Can be prepared and stored in refrigerator 1 day ahead.)*

Preheat oven to 325°F. Pour ½ cup stock into roasting pan. Heavily butter roasting rack and set in pan. Fill turkey loosely with stuffing.

Combine garlic, basil, salt, pepper, rosemary, marjoram and thyme. Rub some of butter over turkey. Sprinkle evenly with herb mixture.

Place turkey breast side down on rack and roast 20 minutes.

Melt remaining butter in small saucepan over medium-low heat. Remove from heat and add wine.

After 20 minutes, baste turkey generously with butter and wine mixture and continue roasting according to wrapper directions. (If there are no directions with turkey, allow about 15 to 18 minutes per pound.) Baste turkey generously with remaining wine mixture and pan juices every 30 minutes or so, checking occasionally to make sure breast skin is not sticking to roasting rack. Add additional ½ cup of stock if more liquid is needed for basting. Cover turkey loosely with foil if it begins to brown too quickly.

During last hour of cooking, turn turkey breast side up. Test for doneness by moving leg; if it wiggles easily, turkey is done. A meat thermometer inserted into thigh should read 180°F to 185°F.

Transfer turkey to large heated platter and cover loosely with foil. Let stand in warm place 15 to 20 minutes before carving and serving. Pass Giblet Gravy with Wine separately.

Venetian Stuffing with Cheese

This stuffing minus the rice makes an excellent dip when blended with a little sour cream or yogurt. Stuffing can be prepared up to 2 days ahead, covered and refrigerated.

Makes enough stuffing for 12- to 15-pound turkey

2 tablespoons (¼ stick) butter
3 green onions, minced
⅔ cup chopped walnuts
1 garlic clove, minced
1 ounce pancetta,* minced
½ teaspoon dried rosemary
¼ teaspoon dried savory
⅛ teaspoon dried thyme
1 pound ricotta cheese

¾ pound fresh Swiss chard *or* spinach, cooked, squeezed dry and finely chopped
1 cup cooked rice
2 ounces freshly grated Parmesan cheese
1½ ounces Fontina cheese, shredded
  Salt and freshly ground pepper

Melt butter in large skillet over medium heat. Add onions; cook 2 minutes.

Stir in walnuts, garlic, pancetta and herbs and continue cooking about 2 minutes, being careful not to burn herbs. Remove from heat and cool.

Transfer to mixing bowl, add remaining ingredients and blend well. Taste and adjust seasoning as desired.

*Available in Italian markets or specialty food shops.

*Grape-Stuffed Cornish Game Hens
with Orange Butter*

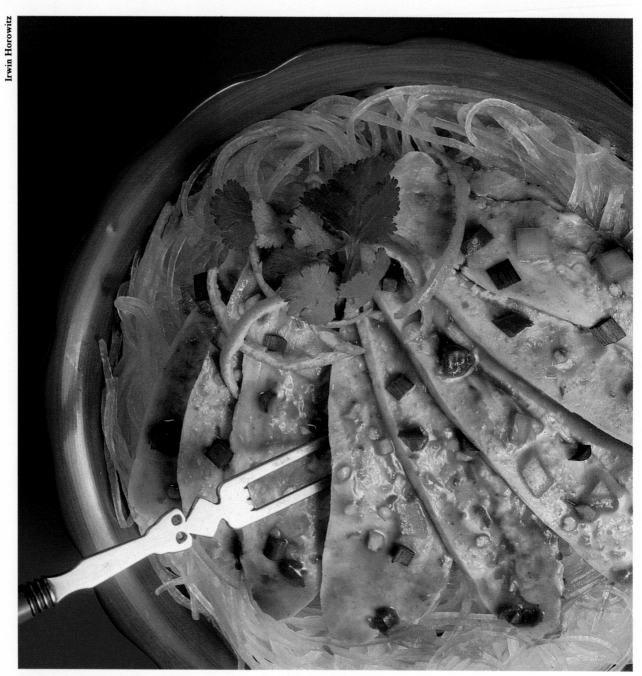

Szechwan Spicy Tangerine Chicken

Victor Scocozza

Butterflied Deviled Chicken

Clockwise from left: Sesame Chicken Salad; Smoked Chicken, Apple and Walnut Salad; Chicken and Melon Salad with Green Chili Mayonnaise

Dan Wolfe

Chicken-Pasta Salad with Fruit

Sticky Chicken

Chicken Sauté with Asparagus and Carrots

Giblet Gravy with Wine

Start the stock base for the gravy while the turkey roasts, then finish it quickly just before bringing the dinner to table. Any leftover gravy can be refrigerated up to 5 days, or frozen up to 3 months in airtight container.

Makes about 2 cups

3 cups water
1½ cups dry white wine
1 large onion, coarsely chopped
1 small carrot, coarsely chopped
1 small celery stalk, including leaves, coarsely chopped
1 garlic clove, crushed
Giblets and neck from turkey, coarsely chopped

Salt and freshly ground pepper

Pan juices from turkey

½ cup water
½ cup Madeira
1 to 2 tablespoons all purpose flour

Combine first 7 ingredients with salt and pepper to taste in medium saucepan. Partially cover and bring to simmer. Stock should reduce to 1½ cups and have intense flavor. *(Can be prepared up to 1 day ahead.)*

When roasted turkey has been transferred to platter, degrease juices in roasting pan. Place pan over high heat. Pour reduced stock through strainer into pan juices. Bring to boil and cook about 2 minutes, stirring and scraping up any browned bits that cling to pan.

Beat together remaining water, Madeira and flour until smooth. Stir into boiling pan juices and continue cooking until gravy is thickened, about 5 minutes. Taste; if sauce seems weak, continue reduction. Adjust seasoning. Pour into heated sauceboat to serve.

Roast Turkey with Apple-Sausage Stuffing

Serve this hearty turkey and stuffing with Brandied Giblet Gravy.

14 to 15 servings

1 18- to 20-pound turkey (if desired, reserve giblets, neck and wing tips for Brandied Giblet Gravy and Poultry Stock; see recipe, page 111)
Salt and freshly ground pepper
Apple-Sausage Stuffing (see following recipe)

½ cup (1 stick) butter, room temperature

Spiced crab apples in heavy syrup (garnish)
Rosemary sprigs (garnish)

Preheat oven to 425°F. Sprinkle turkey neck and body cavities with salt and pepper. Pack cavities loosely with stuffing. Fold neck skin under and secure with skewer. Sew main cavity closed or cover with small piece of aluminum foil. Truss bird. Transfer remaining stuffing to buttered baking dish, cover and refrigerate.

Rub bird with ¼ cup butter; melt remaining butter. Arrange breast side down on rack in large roasting pan. Roast 15 minutes. Baste turkey with melted butter and turn on side. Roast 10 minutes. Repeat with other side.

Turn turkey so breast side is up. Reduce oven temperature to 325°F. Roast turkey until juices run clear when pricked with fork, leg moves easily in its socket and meat thermometer inserted in thickest part of thigh registers 180°F, about 15 to 20 minutes per pound or 3½ to 4 more hours (baste with remaining melted butter, then with pan juices every 30 minutes). If turkey browns too quickly, cover loosely with aluminum foil. Place remaining stuffing in oven during last 40 minutes of cooking time for turkey and bake, covered, 1 hour.

Transfer turkey to serving platter. Cover loosely with aluminum foil. Let stand 20 minutes before carving. Garnish platter with crab apples and rosemary. Pass remaining stuffing.

Apple-Sausage Stuffing

If serving stuffing separately (without turkey), cover and bake 1 hour in 325°F oven.

Makes 14 cups

Pork Sausage with Cognac
1¼ pounds lean pork tenderloin
10 ounces fresh pork fat
1 teaspoon salt
1 teaspoon dried thyme
1 teaspoon dried sage
½ teaspoon freshly grated nutmeg
½ teaspoon freshly ground pepper
¼ teaspoon allspice
¼ cup Cognac

13 to 14 cups ¼-inch day-old French bread cubes (crusts trimmed)

10 tablespoons (1¼ sticks) unsalted butter

2 cups peeled, finely chopped tart green apple (about 1¼ pounds)
1½ cups minced onion
1 cup minced celery
¾ cup minced fresh parsley
1 tablespoon ground sage
1½ teaspoons dried thyme
1 teaspoon salt
Freshly ground pepper

For sausage: Place pork tenderloin and pork fat on baking sheet. Freeze 20 minutes. Quickly cut meat and fat into 1-inch cubes. Pass cubes through meat grinder fitted with fine blade (or have butcher grind meat and fat together twice). Transfer mixture to large bowl. Add salt, thyme, sage, nutmeg, pepper and allspice and mix well. Blend in Cognac. Cover and chill overnight.

Preheat oven to 300°F. Spread cubed French bread on 2 large baking sheets. Bake until brown and dry, stirring frequently, 20 to 30 minutes. Let cool. Transfer to large mixing bowl.

Melt 2 tablespoons butter in large skillet over medium-high heat. Add sausage and cook until no longer pink, 5 to 7 minutes, stirring and pressing with fork occasionally to break up lumps. Add sausage to bread using slotted spoon. Discard fat from skillet.

Melt remaining butter in same skillet over low heat. Add apple, onion and celery and cook until vegetables begin to soften, 5 to 7 minutes, stirring occasionally. Stir in parsley and cook 2 to 3 more minutes. Add mixture to bread and toss gently. Blend in remaining ingredients. Taste and adjust seasoning. Cool completely. Refrigerate before using. *(Can be prepared 1 day ahead.)*

Turkey à l'Orange

8 servings

1 whole turkey breast (4½ to 5 pounds)
1 teaspoon salt
Freshly ground pepper
1 tablespoon unsalted butter
1 tablespoon oil
1½ large shallots, peeled and finely minced

1 teaspoon finely minced orange peel
1½ cups chicken stock
1 cup fresh orange juice
¾ cup Port

1 medium orange, scored, ends cut flat, cut into ⅛-inch slices (garnish)
Watercress sprigs (garnish)

Position rack in center of oven and preheat to 450°F. Using sharp boning knife, remove each turkey breast half from bone in one piece. Remove tendons. Form each piece into tight roll and tie with string. Season with salt and pepper. Melt butter with oil in large ovenproof skillet over medium-high heat. Add turkey and brown on all sides. Remove turkey and set aside. Discard fat from skillet.

Combine shallots and orange peel in processor or blender. With machine running, add stock, orange juice, Port and freshly ground pepper and mix until well blended. Transfer sauce to skillet and bring to boil over high heat. Remove from heat. Add turkey to skillet. Transfer to oven and roast, basting meat and turning occasionally, until thermometer inserted in thickest part of meat registers 170°F, 30 to 35 minutes. Remove turkey from skillet and keep warm. Place skillet over medium-high heat and cook sauce until reduced to 1 cup, 10 to 15 minutes.

Just before serving, discard string from turkey. Cut meat into thin slices and arrange on serving platter with slices overlapping. Drizzle sauce over meat. Garnish with orange and watercress.

Stuffed Turkey Thigh

Boning a turkey thigh is a refinement the pilgrims might not have considered, but it's so easy they could have accomplished it even with limited cutlery. This recipe is also good cold.

2 servings

1 turkey thigh (about 1 pound)
John's Dressing *or* Brown Rice and Mushroom Stuffing (see following recipes)

2 tablespoons (¼ stick) butter, melted

Preheat oven to 350°F. Cut along the thigh lengthwise down to the bone on the inside. Pressing knife against the bone, cut until it is released. Pound meat to flatten as much as possible. Spoon stuffing down center. Bring skin together to enclose filling and tie with string, fastening ends with toothpicks or skewers. Wrap loosely in foil and place in shallow baking pan. Bake 1 hour. Open foil and bake 1 hour longer, basting often with butter and juices until meat is nicely browned. Remove skewers and string and cut into slices.

John's Dressing

Makes enough stuffing for 1 turkey thigh

⅛ pound bulk sausage *or* 2 sausage links, casings removed
¼ cup chopped onion
3 large mushrooms, chopped
½ cup toasted breadcrumbs *or* small bread cubes
¼ cup peeled, chopped tart apple

2 tablespoons chopped walnuts
1 tablespoon minced fresh parsley
Pinch of dried sage
Pinch of dried thyme
Salt and freshly ground pepper
½ beaten egg

Sauté sausage in skillet over medium-high heat until no pink remains. Transfer to bowl using slotted spoon. Add onion and mushrooms to skillet and cook until onion is limp and mushrooms just begin to brown. Add to sausage and toss lightly with breadcrumbs, apple, walnuts and parsley. Season to taste with sage, thyme and salt and pepper. Stir in egg and blend well.

Brown Rice and Mushroom Stuffing

¾ cup chicken stock
⅓ cup brown rice *or* wild rice mix

2 tablespoons olive oil
¼ cup finely diced celery
¼ cup sliced fresh mushrooms
2 green onions, chopped
2 tablespoons minced green bell pepper

2 tablespoons freshly grated Parmesan cheese
1 tablespoon minced fresh parsley
⅛ teaspoon Angostura bitters
½ beaten egg
Salt and freshly ground pepper

Bring stock to boil in small saucepan. Add rice, reduce heat, cover and simmer 45 to 50 minutes. *(Do not lift lid or stir rice during cooking time.)* If you hear a slight crackling sound after 35 or 40 minutes, your rice is drier than usual and has absorbed all stock. Remove from heat and let stand, covered, for remainder of cooking time. Transfer to bowl and fluff with fork.

Heat oil in heavy-bottomed skillet. Add celery, mushrooms, onions and green pepper and cook gently until vegetables are limp. Add to rice and toss lightly. Add cheese, parsley, bitters, egg and salt and pepper and blend well. Cool before stuffing turkey thigh.

Turkey Tonnato

There are several advantages to this method of slicing turkey, since you can cook the turkey breast, cut it into pieces that will fit the feed tube of a processor, and then tuck it into the freezer. When you're ready to complete the recipe, thaw the turkey partially and then use the Medium Slicer for cutting the meat into even pieces. This also stretches the number of servings you can get from the meat. If you find it fits your schedule better you may proceed with the recipe without freezing the meat.

8 servings

1 fresh, whole turkey breast, boned and rolled (about 4 pounds)
1 tablespoon oil (for conventional cooking)
1 onion, quartered
2 carrots (unpeeled), cut into slices or chunks
2 celery stalks, thickly sliced

Basic Mayonnaise (see following recipes)

Tonnato Sauce (see following recipes)

Garnishes
½ large head lettuce, shredded
¼ cup minced fresh parsley
1 hard-cooked egg yolk, riced
2 tablespoons capers, drained
2 small lemons, thinly sliced and scored

With conventional oven: Preheat oven to 325°F. Rub entire surface of turkey with oil. Place in baking dish, surround with vegetables and roast uncovered until meat thermometer registers 170°F, about 1½ to 1¾ hours. Let meat cool. Reserve juices, skimming off fat.

With microwave oven: Arrange vegetables in even layer in glass baking dish. Place turkey breast upside down over vegetables and cook uncovered 17 minutes. Turn turkey right side up and cook another 17 minutes. Turn again, insert meat thermometer, and check reading after 2 minutes. Remove meat thermometer and continue cooking if necessary. Remove from oven when thermometer registers 155°F. *(Meat will continue to cook when it is removed from oven.)* Let meat cool. Reserve juices, skimming off fat.

If slicing with processor: Cut meat into largest size pieces to fit feed tube from bottom so meat will be sliced across the grain. Freeze partially or completely on waxed paper–lined baking sheet. Put frozen meat into airtight plastic bag.

Medium Slicer: Remove turkey from freezer; allow to thaw partially if completely frozen. *Do not slice until knife can easily penetrate meat, but the meat must remain firm; do not let meat soften.* Slice, using firm pressure. Arrange turkey slices in flat dish, cover and refrigerate.

If slicing by hand: Partially freeze meat and slice thinly with very sharp knife.

Prepare Basic Mayonnaise and Tonnato Sauce. Pour Tonnato Sauce over turkey slices and marinate several hours, preferably overnight.

Arrange shredded lettuce on large serving platter. Place turkey on lettuce, garnish with parsley, egg yolk and capers, and surround with lemon slices.

Basic Mayonnaise

This mayonnaise will keep in the refrigerator 2 weeks.

Makes 1½ cups

1 large egg
1 teaspoon fresh lemon juice
1 teaspoon red wine vinegar
1 teaspoon Dijon mustard

1 teaspoon salt
Freshly ground white pepper
1½ cups oil (safflower oil mixed with 3 tablespoons French olive oil)

Combine egg, lemon juice, vinegar, mustard, salt, pepper and 3 tablespoons oil in processor or blender. Let machine run until mixture is thickened. With machine still running, begin adding oil in thin steady stream until mayonnaise thickens. Add remaining oil more quickly. Adjust seasoning to taste.

Tonnato Sauce

This sauce makes a delicious dressing for fresh vegetables.

- 1 small onion, peeled and finely minced
- 1½ cups Basic Mayonnaise
- 1 7-ounce can Italian tuna in olive oil, drained
- 3 flat anchovy fillets, rinsed, patted dry and chopped

- 3 tablespoons fresh lemon juice
- 3 tablespoons capers, drained and crushed
- ¼ to ⅓ cup turkey stock (dilute with water if too strong)
- ¼ cup fresh parsley, minced

Combine all ingredients in processor or blender and mix until well blended.

Turkey Paupiettes with Creamed Chestnuts

4 to 6 servings

Paupiettes
- ½ turkey breast (about 2 pounds) *or* 6 chicken breast halves

Stock
- 2 tablespoons chicken fat *or* butter
- 1 carrot, sliced
- 1 onion, sliced
- 1 celery stalk, sliced
- 1 garlic clove
- 1 bay leaf
- 2 sage leaves
- 3 thyme sprigs *or* 1 teaspoon dried thyme
  Parsley sprigs
  Leek greens (optional)
  Mushroom trimmings (optional)
- 1 15½-ounce can whole chestnuts packed in water, rinsed and drained, *or* 20 large fresh chestnuts, boiled and peeled

- ½ cup whipping cream
  Salt and freshly ground pepper

- 1 cup dry white wine
- ½ cup Port

- 4 tablespoons (½ stick) butter, room temperature
- 1 egg, lightly beaten with salt and freshly ground pepper
- ⅓ cup chestnut flour*
- 2 tablespoons peanut oil

- 1 cup whipping cream
- ¾ teaspoon minced fresh thyme *or* ¼ teaspoon dried
- 2 teaspoons fresh lemon juice
- 2 tablespoons (¼ stick) butter, cut into pieces and chilled
  Minced fresh parsley *or* fresh thyme (garnish)

For paupiettes: Bone turkey breast, reserving all bones and trimmings. Remove skin and reserve. Remove tendon from fillet. With wide part of breast pointed upward, cut 4 to 6 diagonal slices ½ to ¾ inch wide. (If the fillet separates from top part of breast, it may be easier to make horizontal slices following the natural divisions of the meat.) To butterfly, cut horizontally ¾ of the way through the center of each slice, resting one hand on top of turkey while cutting with the other. Open slice; pound between sheets of plastic wrap to flatten. Wrap and chill.

For stock: Melt chicken fat in heavy-bottomed large saucepan over medium heat. Cut up turkey bones and add to pan with all trimmings (except skin), carrot, onion, celery, garlic, bay leaf, sage, thyme, parsley, leek greens and mushroom trimmings. Cook until lightly browned, stirring occasionally, about 10 minutes. Pour in enough water to completely cover vegetable mixture and bring to boil over medium-high heat. Reduce heat and simmer about 4 hours, skimming foam as it rises to surface. Cool slightly. Cover and chill until fat rises to top and solidifies. Discard fat. Strain stock, pressing vegetables to extract all liquid.

Rinse chestnuts thoroughly under cold running water. Bring 1 cup stock to simmer in 1-quart saucepan. Stir in ½ cup cream and bring to simmer again. Add chestnuts and continue cooking uncovered over medium-high heat, stirring frequently, until chestnuts have absorbed most of liquid, about 15 to 20 minutes. Break any remaining large chunks of chestnuts into smaller pieces. Season with salt and pepper to taste.

Pour remaining stock into separate saucepan. Add white wine and Port and boil over high heat until reduced to about 1 cup. Set aside for making sauce.

Preheat oven to 300°F. Divide 2 tablespoons butter among paupiettes, spreading evenly. Divide creamed chestnuts and spread evenly over butter, leaving ½-inch border all around. Starting with small end, roll up and tie securely with string. Dip paupiettes into beaten egg and then dredge in flour, patting to remove excess. Heat remaining 2 tablespoons butter and oil in heavy skillet over medium-high heat.

Add paupiettes and brown well on all sides. Lay reserved skin over paupiettes and cover with piece of buttered parchment paper. Cover skillet with lid. Bake about 15 minutes, until juices run clear when pricked with fork and meat thermometer registers 155°F.

Transfer paupiettes to heated platter. Cut off string. Discard parchment and skin. Drain fat from skillet. Add reduced turkey stock to skillet with cream and thyme and boil over high heat until sauce is reduced and thickened, scraping up any browned bits clinging to bottom of pan. Stir in lemon juice and season to taste with salt and pepper. Whisk in cold butter. Return paupiettes to pan, turning in sauce. Arrange paupiettes on heated plates. Top each with sprinkling of parsley or thyme. Serve immediately.

*Chestnut flour is available in Chinese or Italian markets. You can substitute all purpose flour.

Turkey Valdostana

Café Roma in San Luis Obispo, California, serves this dish with pasta and lightly sautéed zucchini.

6 servings

2 tablespoons all purpose flour
6 slices boneless turkey breast (12 to 14 ounces total), pounded to thickness of ¼ inch
¼ cup (½ stick) unsalted butter
10 medium mushrooms, thinly sliced
¾ cup dry white wine

¾ cup veal stock (preferably homemade)
2 to 3 tablespoons chopped fresh parsley
Freshly ground white pepper
6 thin slices prosciutto
6 thin slices Fontina cheese

Lightly flour turkey slices, shaking off excess. Melt butter in large skillet over low heat. Add turkey and sauté until lightly browned, about 2 minutes on each side. Remove with slotted spatula and set aside. Increase heat to medium low. Add mushrooms and sauté until juices are rendered, about 4 minutes. Add wine and cook until reduced by ¼, about 3 to 4 minutes. Increase heat to medium high. Add veal stock, parsley and pepper and cook until reduced to 1 cup, about 10 minutes. Reduce heat to low. Top each turkey breast with slice of prosciutto and Fontina. Return to skillet and cook just until cheese melts. Transfer with slotted spatula to individual plates. Top each with some of mushroom sauce and serve.

Braised Turkey with Lemon and Cinnamon

4 to 6 servings

4 to 6 tablespoons Greek olive oil
½ cup all purpose flour
2 to 2½ pounds boned and skinned turkey, cut into 1-inch pieces

3 tablespoons Greek olive oil
3 medium onions, chopped
1 garlic clove, minced
⅔ cup undrained canned tomatoes
3 tablespoons tomato paste
2 cinnamon sticks, broken in half, or to taste
2 lemons, or more to taste

1½ teaspoons Greek oregano, or to taste
⅛ teaspoon allspice
2 to 3 cups rich turkey stock or chicken stock

Salt and freshly ground pepper

1 pound ziti (Greek *or* Italian pasta in a hollow rod shape)
4 tablespoons (½ stick) butter
½ cup freshly grated imported Parmesan cheese

Heat 4 tablespoons oil in wok or large skillet over high heat. Place flour in bag, add turkey pieces and shake until well coated. Shake off excess flour. Stir-fry turkey in small batches until lightly browned, adding oil as needed. Remove from heat and set aside.

Heat 3 tablespoons oil in heavy 4- to 5-quart saucepan over high heat. Add onions and cook until golden brown. Stir in garlic and cook another 30 seconds. Reduce heat and stir in tomatoes, tomato paste, cinnamon, lemon juice, pulp and skin of squeezed lemons, oregano and allspice and simmer 5 minutes. Add stock and turkey. Bring to gentle simmer, cover partially and cook 1½ to 2 hours, or until turkey is tender. *Braised Turkey can be prepared to this point up to 4 days ahead and refrigerated, or frozen up to 2 months.*

Taste and adjust lemon juice, cinnamon, oregano and/or salt and pepper. Remove lemon pieces and cinnamon sticks. Skim off excess fat and keep sauce warm while cooking pasta.

Bring 8 quarts of water to boil with 2 tablespoons salt. Break pasta into pieces about 3 inches long. Add to pot and boil, stirring frequently to prevent sticking, until pasta is tender but not mushy. (Greek taste dictates that pasta be cooked a little beyond the al dente stage.) Turn into colander and toss to drain thoroughly. Turn pasta out onto heated large serving platter, dot with butter and toss to coat. Spoon turkey and sauce over pasta and sprinkle with cheese.

Turkey Elegant

3 servings

3 tablespoons butter
¼ cup chopped onion
3 tablespoons all purpose flour
2 cups half and half
½ teaspoon salt
½ teaspoon dried tarragon
1 cup grated Tillamook cheese
2 cups cubed cooked turkey (light and dark meat)

1 2½-ounce can sliced mushrooms, drained

1 avocado
6 baked puff pastry patty shells
6 avocado slices (garnish)
Paprika (garnish)

Melt butter in heavy large skillet over low heat. Add onion and cook until soft, about 10 minutes. Add flour and stir 3 minutes. Add half and half, salt and tarragon and continue cooking until mixture thickens, about 3 to 5 minutes. Add cheese and cook, stirring constantly, until cheese is melted. Stir in turkey and mushrooms and cook until heated through, 5 to 10 minutes.

Peel, pit and dice avocado. Remove skillet from heat and carefully stir in diced avocado. Divide mixture evenly among patty shells. Top each shell with avocado slice. Sprinkle with paprika and serve.

Turkey Mole

2 servings

2 tablespoons oil
2 small turkey thighs (about ¾ pound each)
Chicken stock *or* salted water
1 to 2 dried ancho chilies,* rinsed, stemmed, seeded and coarsely torn

1 medium tomato, peeled, seeded and chopped
6 blanched almonds
½ corn tortilla, chopped
2 tablespoons minced onion
1 teaspoon sesame seed, toasted
¼ to ½ teaspoon dried red pepper flakes, or to taste
⅛ teaspoon aniseed

Pinch of cinnamon
Pinch of ground cloves

¼ ounce unsweetened chocolate
Salt and freshly ground pepper

1 tablespoon sesame seed, toasted

Garnishes
1 medium tomato, peeled, seeded and chopped
½ cup sliced radish
¼ cup minced fresh cilantro (coriander) *or* parsley
¼ cup chopped green chili
1 lime, cut into wedges

Heat oil in medium skillet over medium-high heat. Add turkey and brown on all sides, 4 to 5 minutes each side. Transfer to saucepan just large enough to accommodate (do not clean skillet). Add enough stock or salted water to saucepan to cover turkey. Bring to boil over high heat. Reduce heat to low, cover and simmer gently 1 hour. Meanwhile, combine ancho chilies in bowl with enough hot water to cover. Soak until well softened, 1 hour.

Drain turkey well, reserving cooking liquid. Transfer turkey to baking dish. Drain chilies, discarding soaking liquid; pat dry. Transfer chilies to blender. Add tomato, almonds, tortilla, onion, 1 teaspoon toasted sesame seed and spices; mix to coarse puree.

Heat skillet in which turkey was cooked over medium-high heat. Add chili puree, immediately reduce heat and simmer 5 minutes, stirring constantly. Blend in 1 cup reserved turkey cooking liquid with chocolate and stir until chocolate is melted. Season sauce with salt and pepper. Pour evenly over turkey. *(Can be prepared ahead to this point, covered and refrigerated.)*

Preheat oven to 325°F. Cover dish and bake until turkey is tender when pierced with fork and sauce is consistency of whipping cream, about 1 hour (if sauce is too thick, thin with small amount of reserved turkey cooking liquid). Sprinkle turkey with 1 tablespoon toasted sesame seed.

For garnishes: Place in individual small bowls. Arrange around turkey.

* Also called chili pods.

🐦 *Traditional Turkey in Your Microwave*

During the holidays—or any time—don't limit your microwave to defrosting hors d'oeuvres and reheating leftovers. Think big! Here are some timesaving turkey recipes perfect for any occasion.

Roast Boned Turkey

6 to 8 servings

1 5- to 5½-pound boneless young turkey, rolled and ready to cook
Oil
¼ teaspoon garlic powder, *or* to taste

Salt and freshly ground pepper
Paprika

Set turkey on microwave-safe rack. Rub with oil. Sprinkle with garlic powder, salt and pepper and paprika. Cook on Roast setting (60 percent or 70 percent power) for 30 minutes. Turn roast over. Insert meat probe or microwave-safe thermometer. Continue cooking on Roast until internal temperature reaches 160°F. Remove turkey from microwave and let rest until internal temperature reaches 175°F, about 10 to 15 minutes. Cut into slices and serve.

Turkey Breast on Bed of Garden Vegetables

A boned chicken breast also works well with this recipe. You may choose any or all of the julienne vegetables in combination.

1 to 2 servings

1 medium carrot, cut into julienne slices
1 celery stalk, cut into julienne slices
1 small onion, cut into julienne slices
1 very small potato, cut into julienne slices

1 tablespoon minced fresh parsley
2 tablespoons (¼ stick) butter
Salt and freshly ground pepper
½ turkey breast (skinned if desired)
Paprika

Place first 5 ingredients close together in small au gratin dish just large enough to accommodate all ingredients. Dot top with butter. Season lightly with salt and pepper. Cover with waxed paper and cook on High 7 minutes, stirring once. Set turkey breast on vegetables and sprinkle with paprika. Cover with waxed paper and cook on High 7 to 10 minutes per pound.

Javanese Beer Curry

Unlike the potent curries of India, this sauce, with its undertones of fruit and beer smoothed with cream, enhances rather than masks the delicate flavor of the turkey. Cooked chicken or shrimp can be substituted.

4 servings

3 tablespoons butter
1 medium onion, finely chopped
1 garlic clove, minced
1 teaspoon minced fresh ginger

2 to 4 tablespoons curry powder, or to taste
1 tablespoon all purpose flour
1 cup chicken stock
1 cup beer
1 apple, peeled, cored and diced
2 tablespoons mango chutney

2 teaspoons tomato paste
2 teaspoons honey
Juice of ½ lemon
1 cup whipping cream
3 cups shredded *or* chopped cooked turkey
Salt
Chopped green onion, chopped peanuts and toasted coconut (garnishes)

Melt butter in saucepan over medium heat. Add onion, garlic and ginger and sauté until onion is golden.

Combine curry powder and flour and add to onion, stirring to blend thoroughly. Reduce heat to low and cook 2 to 3 minutes. Add stock, beer, apple, chutney, tomato paste, honey and lemon juice and blend well. Simmer over low heat 25 minutes. Cool slightly, then transfer to processor or blender and puree. Strain through sieve to make perfectly smooth sauce. Return to pan and stir in cream. Add turkey and heat through. Season to taste with salt. Garnish as desired with onion, peanuts and coconut.

Curried Turkey Salad in Brioche

Awaken taste buds with a fresh-tasting chilled sorrel soup. Serve the surprise brioche with an escarole, chicory and endive salad tossed with oil, lemon juice and a touch of Dijon mustard. A chilled Riesling Kabinett would go well.

4 servings

2½ cups cubed cooked turkey
3 tablespoons cored, peeled and finely diced apple (optional)
½ cup mayonnaise
½ cup plain yogurt
2 tablespoons fresh lemon juice
2 teaspoons curry powder
1 teaspoon grated onion
Salt and freshly ground pepper

3 tablespoons chopped green onion
3 tablespoons finely chopped fresh parsley

4 to 8 brioches, hollowed (reserve lids)
Watercress (garnish)
Cherry tomatoes (garnish)

Combine turkey and apple in medium bowl. Blend together mayonnaise, yogurt, lemon juice, curry powder, onion and salt and pepper. Add to turkey and toss to blend. Mix in green onion and parsley and toss lightly. Cover bowl and chill until ready to serve.

Place 1 or 2 brioches on each plate, fill with turkey salad and top with "lid." Garnish with watercress sprigs and cherry tomatoes.

Turkey Salad with Almonds and Ginger

8 to 10 servings

2½ cups water
2 teaspoons salt
1 cup uncooked long-grain brown rice
¼ cup uncooked wild rice

½ cup peanut oil
¼ cup tarragon vinegar
2 tablespoons Dijon mustard
1 tablespoon grated fresh ginger
1 teaspoon freshly ground pepper

1 pound cooked turkey, cut into strips or cubes
2 cups cooked peas
½ cup chopped green onion
½ cup sliced almonds, toasted
¼ cup coarsely chopped red bell pepper

Bring water to boil in medium saucepan over high heat. Add salt and rice. Return to boil, reduce heat, cover and simmer until water is absorbed, about 45 minutes.

Whisk oil, vinegar, mustard, ginger and pepper in large bowl. Stir in rice and remaining ingredients. Serve warm or at room temperature.

3 ❦ Duck and Goose

For most people, the word *succulent* is not usually applied to poultry—except when they are talking about duck or goose. These are, certainly, the richest and juiciest of all birds. Each is unique in flavor, and they are so good that it is astonishing that until recently, few cooks had even one duck or goose recipe in their repertoires. Even today, many people shy away from duck and goose, believing that these special birds present special problems. The "problem" with duck, it is said, is that one bird is too much for two and too little for four. Confronted with this question, one prominent cooking teacher shrugged and said, "Cook *two* ducks, then!" The "problem" with goose, so the story goes, is that it is difficult to prepare and just too fatty; but this is not the case, as the recipe for perfect roast goose on page 81 amply demonstrates—the secret is slow-cooking at a low temperature.

These imaginary problems have never surfaced in France or China, where duck and goose are culinary staples. So it is not surprising that many of the recipes in this chapter are inspired by these two great cuisines. There is, for example, *canard aux baies d'hiver et au citron* (page 70), in which duck is tartly flavored with cranberries and lemon; Fruit-and-Nut-Stuffed Roast Duck (page 77), a variation on a traditional French-African dish; and Duck Breasts with Calvados (page 79), a salute to the great Norman brandy. From China comes crispy Hunan-style duck (page 78); spicy and aromatic deep-fried duck from Szechwan (page 78); and the restaurant favorite, Duck with Plum Sauce (page 69), here served with Chinese pancakes. The French return with a recipe for Braised Goose with Red Wine Sauce (page 82), which includes a "dividend": the goose liver is reserved and matched with pear and Sherry vinegar for a unique and elegant salad (page 80).

Recipes from other countries and other cuisines are featured as well, of course; there is no Franco-Chinese monopoly on duck and goose. And whatever its origin, any of these dishes will provide a special touch to a dinner party.

🍎 Duck

Roast Country Duckling

From the Christiania Inn at Lake Tahoe, California.

4 servings

2 cups (about) oil
4 tablespoons (½ stick) butter
2 4- to 5-pound ducks, fat trimmed from neck and tail
  Onion salt
  Garlic salt
  Salt and freshly ground pepper
½ cup fresh orange juice

1 cup fresh orange juice
1 cup honey
1½ teaspoons soy sauce
½ to ¾ teaspoon cinnamon
  Pinch of ground cloves
  Orange slices (garnish)
  Parsley sprigs (garnish)

Preheat oven to 375°F. Pour oil into large roasting pan to depth of ½ inch. Set aside. Rub 2 tablespoons butter into cavity of each duck. Season cavities with onion salt, garlic salt and salt and pepper. Add ½ cup orange juice to roasting pan. Set ducks in pan breast side up. Cover and roast 1 hour. Uncover, turn ducks over and continue roasting 30 minutes. Turn breast side up and roast another 30 minutes. Transfer ducks to serving platter and let cool at room temperature. *(Can be prepared ahead and refrigerated.)*

    Preheat oven to 450°F. Slice through breastbone of each duck, peel meat back from rib cage and remove ribs, retaining leg and wing bones. Split ducks in half. Combine remaining orange juice, honey, soy sauce, cinnamon and cloves in large saucepan over medium heat. Add duck halves to sauce, turning to coat well. Bring mixture to boil. Remove ducks from sauce and arrange in roasting pan skin side up. Roast 10 minutes to brown. Return ducks to platter. Garnish with orange slices and parsley. Serve with sauce.

Roast Duck in Spicy Sauce

4 servings

1 4½- to 5-pound duck
1 cup water, at boiling point

½ cup salted whole macadamia nuts
2 large garlic cloves, chopped
1 teaspoon ground coriander
½ teaspoon ground ginger

1 cup chicken stock

2 canned whole green chilies

2 tablespoons peanut oil
1 tablespoon fresh lemon juice
  Salt

Preheat oven to 425°F. Pierce duck all over with fork and place on rack in roasting pan. Pour boiling water into pan and roast duck 45 minutes. Remove pan from oven and pour off accumulated fat and juices. Return to oven and roast until duck is cooked, about 45 minutes longer. *(With this method, most of the fat will have rendered into the water in the first 45 minutes, so smoke should not be too much of a problem during second cooking period.)* Let duck cool slightly. Remove all fat, skin and bones; cut meat into small pieces.

    Combine nuts, garlic, coriander, ginger and small amount of stock in processor or blender and mix to smooth paste.

    Wash chilies under cold water; remove any seeds or stems. Pat dry with paper towels and slice into ½-inch squares.

    Heat oil in wok or large skillet. Add nut paste and cook about 30 seconds.

Add chilies and duck and stir-fry another minute. Add remaining chicken stock and lemon juice and cook, stirring constantly, until sauce is slightly thickened, about 5 minutes. Season with salt.

Chinese Duck with Plum Sauce

8 servings

2 4- to 5-pound ducks, all excess fat removed
Salt and freshly ground pepper
2 garlic cloves
2 small pieces fresh ginger
1 cup onion, cut into chunks
2 celery stalks

1 cup ice-cold water

1⅓ cups plum sauce*
⅔ cup bean sauce*

Additional plum sauce, steamed buns *or* Pancakes (see following recipe)

Preheat oven to 400°F. Pat ducks inside and out with paper towels. Rub skin and cavity with salt and pepper, garlic and ginger, then stuff with garlic and ginger pieces, onion and celery.

Place breast side up on rack in shallow pan and roast, pricking skin frequently, 20 minutes. Remove from oven and carefully pour ice water over ducks. Return to oven and roast, pricking skin frequently, 20 minutes longer. Turn and roast another 20 minutes.

Combine plum and bean sauces. Remove ducks from oven and spread some of sauce over backs. Roast 15 minutes. Turn ducks breast side up, spread sauce over and roast another 30 minutes, basting occasionally. Transfer ducks to serving platter and let cool at room temperature. *(Can be prepared ahead and refrigerated.)*

Using kitchen or poultry shears, cut ducks in half lengthwise. With boning knife, cut around joints and remove legs. Cut away wings at joints; remove meat and discard bones. Cut away carcass; discard bones. Lay boned duck flat and slice thinly. Leave legs whole.

To serve, brush duck with additional sauce and reheat to warm through. Serve with dish of plum sauce, steamed buns or Pancakes.

*Available in oriental markets.

Pancakes

Makes 12 to 14 pancakes

1½ cups all purpose flour
¼ teaspoon salt
2 eggs, beaten

1½ cups milk
1 cup water

Sift flour and salt into mixing bowl. Combine eggs, milk and water. Add to dry ingredients and beat until smooth. Cover lightly and let stand at room temperature about 1 hour.

Lightly oil 10-inch skillet (preferably with nonstick finish) and place over low heat. Stir batter; add about ¼ cup to skillet and rotate to spread evenly. Cook until set but not browned; turn and cook on second side. Remove and let cool. Continue until all pancakes are cooked, brushing skillet with oil every 3 or 4 pancakes. Roll each into cylinder and place in serving dish.

Duck with Grapes

6 servings

3 4-pound ducks, all excess fat
   removed, rinsed and patted dry
   Salt and freshly ground pepper
2 cups white wine

½ pound seedless green grapes
½ cup brandy

2 cups chicken stock
1 tablespoon arrowroot dissolved
   in ⅓ cup Port
6 tablespoons (¾ stick) butter

Preheat oven to 400°F. Season ducks with salt and pepper. Truss securely. Set ducks on sides on rack in roasting pan and roast 40 minutes. Discard fat from pan and add ½ cup wine. Turn ducks onto other side and roast 40 minutes, basting every 10 minutes on each side. Discard fat from pan again and add another ½ cup wine. Turn ducks onto backs and continue roasting for 20 minutes, basting several times.

Meanwhile, combine grapes and brandy in small saucepan and bring to boil over medium-high heat. Let boil until liquid is almost evaporated. Remove saucepan from heat.

Transfer ducks to baking dish and keep warm. Remove rack from roasting pan. Add 1 cup wine to pan. Set over medium-high heat and cook, scraping up any browned bits, until liquid is reduced by ⅓. Stir in stock and continue cooking until liquid is reduced by ⅓. Add arrowroot mixture and stir until thickened. Strain into saucepan. Taste and adjust seasoning. Place over low heat and add butter 1 tablespoon at a time, stirring until well blended. Add reserved grapes.

Carve ducks and arrange on platter or individual serving plates. Spoon sauce over top. Serve immediately.

Duck with Cranberry and Lemon Sauce

*Traditionally made with
red currants, this recipe
calls for more readily available fresh cranberries
instead.*

6 servings

2 tablespoons (¼ stick) butter
3 5-pound ducks, wing tips and
   necks chopped into 1½-inch
   pieces
1 quart rich veal stock

1½ cups fresh cranberries
1 teaspoon grated lemon peel

1 cup (scant) water
3 tablespoons currant jelly (or
   more)

¼ cup ruby Port
   Fresh lemon juice
   Salt and freshly ground pepper
   Peel of 2 lemons, cut into fine
   julienne slices and blanched 10
   minutes
   Watercress sprigs (garnish)

Melt butter in heavy large saucepan over medium-high heat. Add duck wings and necks and sauté until deep golden. Discard butter from skillet. Add veal stock and bring to boil. Reduce heat to low and simmer until reduced to 1 to 1¼ cups, about 1½ hours. *(Duck essence can be prepared several days ahead and refrigerated or frozen for several months.)*

Preheat oven to 325°F. Crush 12 cranberries. Place 4 crushed cranberries and pinch of lemon peel into cavity of each bird. Truss birds. Set on rack in large roasting pan. Roast until juices run clear when pricked with fork, about 2 to 2½ hours, tilting ducks at regular intervals to drain juice from cavities into pan.

Meanwhile, combine remaining cranberries in medium saucepan with water and 3 tablespoons currant jelly. Cook over low heat until just tender, about 3 minutes. Reserve 18 uniform berries for garnish. Return remainder to heat and continue cooking berries until completely softened, about 7 minutes. Press mixture through fine sieve to remove skins. *(Cranberry puree can be prepared several days ahead to this point and refrigerated.)* Blend about ⅓ cup cranberry puree (or to taste) into reserved duck essence. Set sauce aside.

Remove ducks from roasting pan and keep warm. Degrease pan. Place over medium-high heat, add Port and stir, scraping up any browned bits. Blend pan juices into sauce. Puree sauce in blender or processor until smooth. Strain into small saucepan. Taste and adjust seasoning with currant jelly, lemon juice and salt and pepper. Stir in lemon peel julienne. Reheat sauce. Arrange 1 leg and half of duck breast on side of each heated plate. Spoon sauce over. Garnish with watercress and reserved berries.

Roast Duck with Port and Chestnut Sauce

An elegant party dish, especially well suited for a festive dinner during the holiday season. To start, serve a light scallop mousse accompanied by a sauce verte. Finish with an apple meringue pudding or an apple tarte. Suggested wine: California Cabernet Sauvignon.

4 to 6 servings

1 cup water
½ cup golden raisins
⅓ cup Port

2 4½- to 5-pound ducks, all excess fat removed, rinsed and patted dry
Salt and freshly ground white pepper
2 tablespoons (¼ stick) unsalted butter

1 teaspoon vegetable oil

2 medium onions, quartered
2½ cups duck stock *or* beef stock

12 to 14 peeled fresh chestnuts*

1 tablespoon arrowroot dissolved in a little Port

Watercress sprigs (garnish)

Bring water to boil in small saucepan. Add raisins and simmer until plumped, about 5 minutes. Drain well. Transfer to small bowl, add Port and set aside.

Preheat oven to 400°F. Season ducks with salt and pepper. Truss securely. Heat butter with oil in heavy large skillet over medium-high heat. Add ducks and brown on all sides, pricking well with fork to let fat drain out.

Place onions in bottom of roasting pan. Add rack, set ducks on top and roast 15 minutes. Reduce oven temperature to 350°F. Prick ducks again, turn on their sides and continue roasting, pricking every 15 minutes and then basting with 1 cup total of the duck stock, until done, about 2½ hours.

Transfer ducks to baking dish and keep warm. Remove rack and as much fat as possible from roasting pan. Add chestnuts (if using fresh) and bake until fork-tender, about 15 minutes. Remove chestnuts with slotted spoon and set aside. Degrease pan juices again and place roasting pan over direct heat. Cook, loosening browned bits with slotted spoon. Strain into saucepan, pressing with spoon to extract juices. Add undrained raisins and cook until liquid is reduced to 2 tablespoons. Add remaining stock and continue cooking until reduced to about 1 cup.

Meanwhile, quarter nuts; set aside.

Stir arrowroot mixture into sauce and whisk until thickened. Add chestnuts.

Carve ducks and arrange on platter. Spoon some of sauce over top; pour remaining sauce into gravy boat. Garnish platter with watercress and serve.

*Canned chestnuts may be substituted. Add them to finished sauce and cook over very low heat until mixture is just heated through.

❦ Tips for a Perfect Duck

- A meaty 5-pound duck is usually adequate for 3 people.
- To select a duck, the fresh-versus-frozen controversy isn't the primary one; frozen ducks can be just as flavorful as fresh ones. It is important, though, to buy according to a brand name you have tried and like.
- Of the three varieties of ducks available—mallard, Muscovy and white Pekin (or Long Island)—the Pekin is most easily obtained. The variety isn't as important as who puts the brand on it; try various brands until you find one to your taste.
- If the duck is frozen, defrost it in the refrigerator overnight.
- Before cooking, remove fat pads from the interior of the bird; cut off all but 1 inch of neck flap; tuck wings under back to elbows and form a triangle.
- Glaze *before* roasting for a rich, mahogany-colored skin. Do not glaze again during the roasting process.
- Do not truss the bird; this will prevent fat from being rendered.
- To roast, set bird on a cake rack or wire rack well above a drip pan. (If you allow the bird to rest in the pan during roasting, the underside will not be crisp.)
- To test for doneness, prick the skin: If the juices have a pinkish cast, the meat is rare; if the juices run clear, the meat is well done.
- To serve, it is not necessary to carve the bird in the traditional way. Instead, it can be cut into quarters or halves with poultry shears.

Perfect Roast Duck

Although the simplest way to achieve crisp, richly browned duck is to cook it until all the fat has dripped away, this usually results in overcooked meat. The 2-step preparation below guarantees the same desirable crispness outside, but will yield firm, juicy and flavorful meat with a tinge of pink at the bone. If you prefer the meat more well-done, reduce oven temperature to 350°F after 20 minutes and cook for 30 minutes longer.

Step 1—Steaming

- Prick duck skin all over.
- Put steamer or rack in large deep pot and add 1 inch of stock or water. Set duck, breast side up, on steamer.

❦

- Bring liquid to simmer, then cover and steam duck gently 1 hour.
- At end of hour, remove duck and carefully pat dry; do not tear skin (save broth for your stockpot).

Step 2—Roasting

- Place 1 rack in middle of oven and second rack in lower third position. Preheat oven to 425°F.
- Prick duck all over once more and brush with **Honey-Soy Wash:** Mix ¼ cup hot water, 2 tablespoons dark soy sauce and 1 tablespoon honey (this makes enough to brush over 2 or 3 ducks).
- Set duck on cake rack or wire rack or directly on oven rack; place large drip pan on bottom rack.
- Roast duck for exactly 20 minutes (it will be mahogany brown).
- Remove duck from oven and let rest 10 minutes before carving. Sauce as desired.

Perfect Disjointed Duck

A method that permits you to cook duck ahead and finish it just before serving is to disjoint the bird and sauté it. Here are 2 variations.

To disjoint duck:

Lay duck on its side and carve off leg and thigh at thigh joint. Repeat on other side. Using poultry shears, cut down center of breast and along one side of wishbone. Press down until ribs crack in middle. Continue cutting until breast is free, leaving wing attached. The few bones adhering to the breast meat will help it hold its shape during cooking, so do not remove them. Repeat on other side.

Trim ragged bits of bone, skin and fat from the two breast pieces, legs and thighs. (Use backbone and ribs in stock.)

To sauté:

Heat a nonstick pan briefly over medium heat. Add legs, skin side down, and sauté until puffed on top, crispy brown on bottom and nearly all fat has been rendered, about 20 minutes. Turn and brown briefly on other side. Remove legs and pour off fat. Add breasts, skin side down, and sauté until browned— 10 minutes at most. Do not brown breasts on skinless side.

Duck with Vinegar Sauce (Caneton au Vinaigre)

4 to 6 servings

2 4½- to 5-pound ducks, partially thawed in refrigerator (ice crystals should remain)
½ pound slab bacon, cut into pieces 1 × ⅓ inch

2 teaspoons dried tarragon, *or* to taste
½ teaspoon salt
½ teaspoon freshly ground pepper
⅓ cup Sherry wine vinegar *or* fine wine vinegar, or to taste

2 tablespoons (¼ stick) unsalted butter
7 tablespoons coarsely chopped shallot
2 tablespoons all purpose flour
2 cups duck Demi-glace (see recipe, page 109)
1 cup Crème Fraîche (see recipe, page 22)

Freshly cooked and buttered noodles

Disjoint ducks; prick skin well. Sauté legs in large nonstick pan, pricking skin frequently to remove as much fat as possible, until golden brown, about 15 minutes. Turn and let cook another 5 minutes. Remove legs. Pour off fat. Add breasts and cook until golden. Remove. Add bacon pieces to pan and cook until well browned. Remove and set aside separate from duck. Discard fat.

Return legs to pan skin side up; top with breasts. Sprinkle with tarragon, salt and pepper. Add vinegar. Cover pan with foil, then lid. Braise slowly until thighs are tender, about 30 to 45 minutes. Remove and discard skin and any excess fat. Arrange pieces in serving casserole and keep warm. Skim fat from pan and reserve cooking juices.

For sauce, melt butter in medium saucepan over medium heat. Add shallot and sauté briefly. Sprinkle with flour and cook, stirring constantly 1 to 2 minutes, to make a light roux. Add demi-glace and cooking juices and simmer gently. Blend in Crème Fraîche and continue simmering *(do not boil)* until sauce is reduced and flavorful. Taste and add more tarragon or vinegar if desired.

Add half of bacon pieces to duck. Add sauce and toss well. Sprinkle with remaining bacon. Serve with noodles.

Honey-brined Smoked Duck

Here's one for the barbecue specialist. Use soaked hickory chips for best flavor.

4 to 6 appetizer servings

Brine
4 quarts water
½ cup sugar
⅓ cup salt (preferably rock salt *or* coarse salt)
⅓ cup honey
10 whole cloves

2 teaspoons crushed black peppercorns

1 4½- to 5-pound duck

Dark bread (optional)

For brine: Combine first 6 ingredients in Dutch oven and simmer 5 minutes. Let cool to room temperature.

Place duck in large deep pot. Add brine. Weight duck with plates to keep submerged. Cover and chill at least 5 days.

Prepare barbecue by placing large drip pan in bottom and surrounding with briquets (about 16 to a side). When briquets are quite hot, separate slightly and throw on generous handful of hickory chips. Place grill on barbecue and set duck over pan. Cover and adjust air vents so they are about ⅔ open.

Smoke duck about 3 hours, adding hickory chips every 30 minutes until about 3 cups have been used. When duck leg moves easily and juices begin to run clear when pricked with a fork, bird is done. *(The brine will give flesh a pinkish cast but, like ham, it will be fully cooked and still retain color.)*

Remove duck. Wrap well in foil and let stand until cool. Cut into thin slices and serve on dark bread if desired.

Pan-broiled Duck with Daikon Dipping Sauce (Okaribayaki)

This is traditionally served at the emperor's hunting parties, where it is prepared in a heavy iron skillet set over a charcoal fire. It is equally good made in an electric skillet. Each guest cooks duck and vegetables at the table.

8 servings

2 4- to 5-pound ducks
4 to 6 egg whites, lightly beaten

6 tablespoons Japanese soy sauce
2 green onions, chopped

8 dried mushrooms (preferably shiitake),* softened 30 minutes in warm water to cover, drained and squeezed dry
4 medium carrots

2 sweet potatoes, peeled and cut into ¼-inch slices
1 green bell pepper, cored, seeded and cut into 1-inch-long julienne strips

4 tablespoons oil
Daikon Dipping Sauce (see following recipe)

Discard skin, bone and tendon from duck breasts, legs and thighs (reserve remaining duck and livers for another use). Cut boned breasts into narrow strips and set aside. Put leg and thigh meat through fine blade of grinder twice, or mince in processor. Transfer ground duck to bowl. Add egg whites and blend thoroughly. Form into 1-inch balls. Cover and refrigerate.

Combine soy sauce and green onions in serving bowl and set aside.

Remove and discard hard stems from soaked mushrooms, then cut each mushroom in half. To cut carrots into oblique slices ¾ to 1 inch thick, make one diagonal cut, then roll carrot a quarter turn and slice parallel to first cut. Continue rolling and cutting remaining carrots in same manner. Bring saucepan of water to rapid boil over high heat. Add carrots and blanch 5 minutes. Drain in colander, then rinse with cold water to stop cooking process. Drain carrot slices well.

Arrange duck strips, duck meatballs, mushroom halves, carrots, sweet potatoes and green pepper attractively on 2 platters. *(Can be prepared ahead, covered with plastic wrap and refrigerated.)*

At serving time, add 2 tablespoons oil to each of 2 electric skillets or heavy skillets placed on tableside burners. Preheat electric skillet to 375°F; preheat non-electric skillet over high heat for 5 minutes. Have each guest dip duck strip, meatball or piece of vegetable into soy sauce mixture using long chopsticks or fondue forks. Cook food 2 to 3 minutes, remove from skillet and dip into sauce.

*Available in oriental markets.

Daikon Dipping Sauce

Makes about 2½ cups

2 cups grated daikon (Japanese white radish) *or* white turnip
½ cup Japanese soy sauce

2 egg yolks
Salt

Combine all ingredients and beat well. Serve in bowl or individual dishes.

Royal Duck Curry (Gaeng Pet)

Asians, who are known to be frugal in the kitchen, generally eat fowl with the bone in, with the exception of Chinese-influenced stir-fried dishes that use bone-less chicken. Bone-in is more economical and more flavorful. Serve with steamed white rice.

6 to 8 servings

Chili-Garlic Spice Paste
9 dried red chilies *or* 1 tablespoon ground red pepper
1 tablespoon coriander seed
1 teaspoon black peppercorns
1 teaspoon caraway seed
4 whole cloves *or* ¼ teaspoon ground cloves
10 medium garlic cloves, minced
4 medium shallots, minced
1 tablespoon vegetable oil (or more)
2 teaspoons shrimp paste (kapee)* *or* 2 teaspoons anchovy paste
1 lemongrass stalk, minced *or* 2 teaspoons finely minced lemon peel
1 teaspoon salt
1 teaspoon freshly grated nutmeg
½ teaspoon turmeric
1 2-inch piece fresh ginger, minced
Peel of 1 lime, minced

1 3-pound duck, all excess fat removed

Curry
3 tablespoons vegetable oil

1 quart thick coconut milk *or* 3 cups whole milk mixed with 1 cup half and half and flavored with 1 teaspoon coconut extract
¼ cup fish sauce (nam pla)*
6 fresh citrus leaves, torn in half, *or* 6 dried citrus leaves
6 red serrano chilies, seeded and slivered, *or* 2 large jalapeño chilies, seeded and slivered
2 tablespoons fresh basil leaves, minced, *or* 1 tablespoon dried
2 tablespoons fresh minced cilantro (coriander) leaves
Additional fish sauce (optional)

For paste: Combine chilies, coriander seed, peppercorns, caraway seed and cloves in mortar and crush to powder. Transfer to processor or blender. Add garlic, shallots, 1 tablespoon oil, shrimp paste, lemongrass, salt, nutmeg, turmeric, ginger and lime peel and mix until as smooth as possible *(paste will be slightly coarse)*, adding up to 1 tablespoon more oil as necessary to facilitate turning of blades. Set aside.

Set duck breast side up on work surface. Bend 1 leg down and away from body until skin between leg and body is stretched taut. Using long, heavy, very sharp knife, or boning knife and heavy sharp meat cleaver, or kitchen scissors, nick taut skin, then continue to cut slit parallel to body so that leg is released and flat on work surface. Bend leg backward until end of thighbone pops upward and is visible. Carefully cut around thigh joint, then between bones at joint; leg will cut loose. Repeat with remaining duck leg.

Cut skin between thigh and drumstick to expose joint. Bend leg back and forth to locate exact position of joint. Cut between bones and through flesh and skin to separate thigh and drumstick. Chop off end of drumstick by pressing cleaver into place, then hitting top edge of cleaver sharply with hammer. Repeat with other drumstick. Chop thighs and drumsticks into bite-size pieces using cleaver and hammer.

Locate shoulder joint where wing is attached to body and make incision in skin in same manner as for legs. Expose joint, then cut each wing from body in similar style. Cut off wing tips. Halve wings using cleaver and hammer.

Stand duck carcass up on its neck. The front (or breast portion) is only attached to the back by the ribs. Follow curved rib line and cut right through between breast and back, leaving flesh on breast side. Repeat on other side and, with hands, pull front section away from back. Cut off excess fat and skin (only small amount is needed to flavor sauce when cooking).

Lay breast outer side down on work surface. Cut in half lengthwise using large knife or cleaver. Chop each half into 3 pieces crosswise using cleaver and hammer. Chop back portion into bite-size pieces using cleaver and hammer. Carefully remove any bone fragments. Set duck pieces aside.

For curry: Heat oil in large wok or saucepan over medium heat. Add 3 tablespoons reserved spice paste and stir-fry 3 minutes, scraping bottom frequently so paste does not stick. Add duck pieces and stir to coat thoroughly. Reduce heat to low. Cover saucepan and cook 10 minutes, stirring occasionally to prevent sticking and burning.

Degrease surface of duck mixture with bulb baster and paper towels. Stir in coconut milk, fish sauce and citrus leaves. Increase heat to medium high and bring sauce to boil. Reduce heat and simmer until duck is tender and meat begins to draw back from bone, about 20 minutes. Transfer duck to heated plate using slotted spoon. Degrease surface of sauce. Stir in half of chilies, basil and cilantro. Simmer sauce until reduced by ⅓, about 10 minutes. Taste and season with additional fish sauce if desired. Return duck to wok and heat through. Transfer to dish. Sprinkle with remaining chilies, basil and cilantro and serve.

*Available in oriental markets.

Fruit-and-Nut-Stuffed Roast Duck
(Canard el Caliph)

Serve with saffron rice.

4 servings

1½ cups dry white wine
¼ cup honey
½ pound dried pitted apricots, snipped into halves or quarters
½ pound pitted dates, coarsely chopped
2 apples, peeled, cored and chopped
1 small onion, finely chopped
1 cup coarsely chopped walnuts *or* shelled pistachios
⅓ cup fresh lemon juice

1 tablespoon cinnamon
1 teaspoon allspice
1 teaspoon salt
½ teaspoon ground cumin
½ teaspoon freshly ground pepper
1 4½- to 5-pound duck
  Stock *or* water

Honey-Soy Wash
¼ cup hot water
2 tablespoons dark soy sauce
1 tablespoon honey

Combine wine and ¼ cup honey in small saucepan and bring to simmer. Add apricots and set sauce aside.

Combine next 10 ingredients in large bowl. Drain apricots (reserve liquid), add to bowl and toss lightly. Stuff duck as full as possible; set remaining stuffing aside. Sew vent shut; prick skin well. Steam over stock or water (see box, page 72) for 1 hour.

Place 1 rack in middle of oven and second rack in lower third. Preheat oven to 425°F. Remove duck from steamer and let cool briefly. Carefully blot dry and prick skin again.

For honey-soy wash: Combine ingredients and brush duck with some of wash, then glaze with some of reserved honey-wine sauce. Set duck on cake rack or wire rack or directly on oven rack; place large drip pan on bottom rack. Roast ducks 20 minutes. Transfer to oval gratin dish. Reduce oven temperature to 350°F.

Spoon remaining stuffing around duck and brush with honey-wine sauce. Roast another 15 to 30 minutes, or until desired degree of doneness and crispness is reached. Remove from oven and let rest 10 minutes. Carve duck at table and serve with remaining sauce.

Szechwan Duck

This fragrant, sophisticated dish is one of the most delicious in all of the Chinese cuisines. It is the Szechwan equivalent of Peking Duck and is often served at Chinese banquets as the climax of the meal.

3 main-course servings

1 5- to 6-pound duck, all excess fat removed

Marinade
1 stick cinnamon, broken into about 4 ½-inch pieces
2 tablespoons coarse salt
1 tablespoon Szechwan peppercorns*
1 star anise* (8 pods)

4 slices ginger, crushed
1 green onion, cut into 2-inch lengths and crushed

1 tablespoon light soy sauce
2 tablespoons all purpose flour

6 cups oil

Garnish
1 tablespoon light soy sauce
2½ teaspoons sesame oil*
½ teaspoon sugar
⅛ teaspoon freshly ground white pepper
3 cups watercress, tough stems removed

Rinse duck; drain and pat dry. Remove tips from wings and discard.

For marinade: Combine cinnamon, salt, peppercorns and star anise in small skillet and toast until salt is slightly browned. Crush spices lightly.

Rub ginger and green onion over entire cavity of duck; reserve bits of ginger and onion. Rub salt-spice mixture over skin and in cavity. Place ginger and onion in cavity. Place duck in bowl and cover tightly, or wrap in foil. Chill 24 hours.

Brush salt mixture from skin and remove ginger and onion from cavity. Prick skin all over. Add 1 inch water to large deep pot. Set steamer or rack inside. Place duck on plate, breast side up, set in steamer and bring water to boil. Cover tightly and steam duck gently, pricking frequently until all fat has drained out and duck is tender, about 1 hour. Remove duck (reserve accumulated liquid for later use if desired); let cool.

Rub entire surface of duck with soy sauce and let dry thoroughly. Rub flour over and let stand 10 minutes.

Heat oil in wok to 350°F. Slowly lower duck, breast side down, into oil. Deep fry until golden brown and crisp, turning duck to ensure even browning, about 10 to 15 minutes. Carefully remove with large tongs and let excess oil drain off.

To prepare garnish: While duck is cooking, combine soy sauce, oil, sugar and white pepper and mix well. Toss thoroughly with watercress and set aside. Line serving platter with watercress and arrange duck on top. Slice or chop duck into pieces at table.

*Available in oriental markets.

Hunan-style Crispy Duck

For enthusiasts of crisp duck, this tops all. Serve Chinese style by cutting duck into bite-size squares with a cleaver.

4 servings

1 4½- to 5-pound duck

Marinade
6 slices fresh ginger, peeled
5 green onions
3 tablespoons salt
1 tablespoon rice wine *or* dry Sherry

1 teaspoon freshly ground pepper
½ star anise*

Stock *or* water
1 tablespoon soy sauce

Peanut oil

Prick duck skin all over.

For marinade: Pulverize 6 marinade ingredients in blender. Rub over duck inside and out. Let duck stand at room temperature for 30 minutes to absorb marinade flavors.

Steam over stock or water (see box, page 72) for 1 hour. Remove and let cool slightly. Carefully pat dry, then rub skin with soy sauce.

Pour about 3 inches oil in Dutch oven and heat to 400°F. Carefully lower duck breast side up into oil. Cover and fry 10 minutes. Turn breast side down and fry 10 minutes longer. Remove with large tongs and let excess oil drain off. Cut into small squares and serve.

* Available in oriental markets.

Duck with Apples and Cider

For alternate presentation: After duck pieces are braised, let cool until easy to handle. Remove major bones and cut meat into large chunks. Thread on skewers. When ready to serve, reheat in oven or under broiler. Arrange apples in dish, place skewers on top and drizzle with sauce.

4 to 6 servings

2 4½- to 5-pound ducks, partially thawed in refrigerator (ice crystals should remain)
2 cups hard cider *or* apple cider

4 Golden Delicious apples
2 tablespoons (¼ stick) unsalted butter, room temperature

¼ cup sugar

2 cups duck Demi-glace (see recipe, page 109)
1 cup whipping cream
Salt and freshly ground pepper

Following directions in box on page 72, disjoint ducks. Sauté over high heat until browned. After discarding rendered fat, return duck pieces to pan with legs on bottom and breasts on top. Add ½ cup cider, cover and braise slowly until thighs are tender, 30 to 45 minutes. Keep warm.

Meanwhile, preheat oven to 400°F. Peel apples; halve vertically and core. Place on buttered baking sheet. Brush with butter and sprinkle with sugar. Bake until cooked but not mushy, and lightly flecked with brown, about 15 minutes.

For sauce: Melt demi-glace in medium saucepan. Add remaining 1½ cups cider and simmer until reduced by about half. Add cream and continue simmering until sauce is rich and velvety. Season to taste with salt and pepper.

To serve, arrange duck pieces alternately with apple halves in oval gratin dish. Drizzle with some of hot sauce and pass remaining sauce separately.

Duck Breasts with Calvados

2 servings

4 half duck breasts, skinned and boned
Salt and freshly ground pepper
6 tablespoons (¾ stick) unsalted butter

1 tart apple, peeled, cored and thinly sliced

1 tablespoon minced shallot
¼ cup Calvados
¼ cup dry white wine
¼ cup duck stock *or* chicken stock

Season duck with salt and pepper. Melt 1 tablespoon butter in heavy skillet over medium heat. Add duck and brown well on all sides, about 3 minutes per side. Transfer to heated platter; set aside and keep warm.

Melt 1 tablespoon butter in same skillet. Add apple and sauté until tender, about 6 minutes. Add to duck and keep warm. Melt another tablespoon butter in same skillet. Stir in shallot and cook until tender. Add Calvados, wine and stock and cook until reduced by half. Blend in remaining butter to thicken. Taste and adjust seasoning. Slice duck breasts diagonally and arrange over apples. Spoon some of sauce over top; pour remainder into sauceboat. Serve hot.

Duck Salad

2 servings

1 whole duck breast

2 tablespoons red wine vinegar
½ cup duck stock

1 tablespoon unsalted butter
¼ pound mushrooms, preferably Japanese tree mushrooms
1 tablespoon minced shallot
1 tablespoon minced fresh tarragon

1 tablespoon unsalted butter

4 slices French bread cut ½ inch thick
1 garlic clove, cut in half

1 head curly endive, washed and crisped
¼ cup Vinaigrette Dressing (see following recipe)
3 medium tomatoes, blanched, peeled, seeded and cut into ¼-inch dice

Preheat oven to 550°F. Prick duck breast with fork. Place fat side down on rack over broiling pan and roast until outside is crisp but inside is still pink, about 20 minutes. Keep duck breast warm but let stand at least 5 minutes before slicing.

Pour off grease and deglaze pan with vinegar. Add duck stock. Bring to boil over direct heat and cook until liquid is reduced by about ⅔.

Meanwhile, melt 1 tablespoon butter in 10-inch skillet over medium-high heat. Add mushrooms, shallot and tarragon and sauté 2 to 3 minutes.

Just before ready to serve, melt remaining butter in skillet and sauté bread slices on both sides until very crisp. Remove and rub with garlic clove.

Toss endive with vinaigrette. Mound in center of serving plate. Surround with tomatoes, sautéed bread and mushrooms. Slice duck breast against the grain and arrange over endive. Pour deglazed sauce over duck and serve immediately.

Vinaigrette Dressing

1 tablespoon Sherry wine vinegar
1 tablespoon fresh lemon juice
1 tablespoon Dijon mustard, or more to taste
1 tablespoon chopped fresh chives *or* chopped fresh tarragon

Salt and freshly ground pepper
6 to 8 tablespoons almond oil *or* walnut oil

Combine vinegar, lemon juice, mustard, chives and salt and pepper in small bowl and mix well. Whisk in oil.

 Goose

Goose Liver and Pear Salad

4 servings

1 goose liver, *or* 2 duck livers *or* chicken livers
Milk

2 tablespoons Sherry wine vinegar
3 tablespoons walnut oil
Salt and freshly ground pepper

2 tablespoons (¼ stick) unsalted butter

Lettuce leaves
1 large unpeeled pear, cored and cut into julienne slices

Combine liver in small bowl with enough milk to cover. Cover tightly and refrigerate overnight.

Place vinegar in another small bowl. Gradually whisk in walnut oil. Season dressing with salt and pepper.

Just before serving, drain liver, discarding milk. Pat dry. Melt butter in heavy small skillet over medium heat. Add liver and cook, turning once, until browned on outside and pink within, about 3 to 4 minutes total. Remove skillet from heat. Cut liver diagonally into thin slices.

Arrange lettuce leaves on individual salad plates. Arrange pear decoratively over lettuce. Top with liver slices. Spoon dressing evenly over salads.

Roast Goose

The appearance of a goose with its crackling golden skin guarding the succulent meat beneath always signals a celebration. Yet many cooks shy away from goose, considering it difficult to cook and too fatty in the bargain. They don't know what they're missing. By carefully removing all the excess fat and roasting the goose at a low temperature, you won't have any problems. What's more, the rendered goose fat is a special dividend to be saved and treasured. It can be frozen and used later to give pâtés and terrines an exquisite flavor, and you won't believe what it does for sautéed potatoes.

8 servings

1 12- to 14-pound goose *or* 2 smaller geese, 6 to 7 pounds each
3 cups water
1 medium onion, sliced
1 large carrot
1 celery stalk, including leaves
  Salt
5 to 6 whole peppercorns

1 or 2 lemons, halved

Apple-Sage Dressing (see following recipes)

Lemon–Red Currant Glaze (see following recipes)

Rendered goose fat *or* butter

1 tablespoon butter
1 tablespoon all purpose flour
  Freshly ground pepper

Tangerine baskets filled with chutney, frosted grapes and watercress sprigs (garnish)

Remove neck and giblets from goose, reserving liver, and place in medium saucepan with water, onion, carrot, celery, salt to taste and peppercorns. Bring to boil, then reduce heat and simmer 1½ hours, or until giblets are tender. Allow to cool, then chop.

Remove all excess fat from goose (render and reserve for future use if desired). Rinse goose and pat dry. Rub inside and out with lemon halves and sprinkle cavity with salt to taste.

Prepare Apple-Sage Dressing.

Preheat oven to 325°F. Lightly stuff body and neck cavity of goose, being sure not to pack too firmly, since dressing will expand during cooking. Place any extra dressing in casserole dish to be heated with goose during last hour of cooking. Truss goose and skewer or sew opening. Place breast side up on rack in large roasting pan and roast until thigh meat feels soft and joint moves easily, about 16 to 20 minutes per pound. As goose cooks, remove rendered fat with bulb baster and set aside.

About 30 minutes before goose is done, paint with Lemon-Red Currant Glaze. When goose is done, transfer to warm platter and let stand 15 minutes.

Cut liver into 4 pieces and sauté in small amount of reserved rendered fat or butter until browned on outside but still pink within. Chop for use in gravy.

Skim fat from roasting pan, add giblet stock and bring to boil over direct heat, scraping to remove browned bits from bottom of pan. Mix butter and flour together to form a paste and add to stock. Season to taste with salt and pepper and stir in chopped giblets and liver.

Garnish platter with tangerine baskets filled with chutney, frosted grapes and sprigs of watercress.

Apple-Sage Dressing

6 tablespoons (¾ stick) butter	1 cup chopped walnuts
1 cup chopped onion	¼ cup chopped fresh parsley
½ cup chopped celery	2 eggs, beaten
5 to 6 cups cubed bread	1 teaspoon ground dried sage
1½ cups peeled and diced tart apple	1 teaspoon salt
1 cup cooked ham, cut into ¼- to ½-inch cubes	½ teaspoon dried thyme
	½ teaspoon freshly ground pepper

Melt butter in medium skillet over medium-high heat. Add onion and celery and sauté until softened. Transfer to large bowl and mix in bread. Stir in remaining ingredients and blend well.

Lemon–Red Currant Glaze

Juice of 1 lemon	½ cup red currant jelly

Combine ingredients in small saucepan and heat until melted.

Braised Goose with Red Wine Sauce

Any remaining braising liquid can be used with poultry or pasta, or as base for soup.

4 to 6 servings

½ cup oil
2 medium onions, sliced
2 carrots, sliced
2 celery stalks, sliced
2 garlic cloves
½ teaspoon dried thyme
1 bay leaf
1 8- to 10-pound goose, including neck, heart and gizzard (trim and reserve wing tips; reserve liver for Goose Liver and Pear Salad, see recipe, page 80)

½ cup chopped fresh parsley

Salt and freshly ground pepper

5 tablespoons all purpose flour
4 cups chicken stock
2½ cups dry red wine

Watercress sprigs and brandied fruit (optional garnishes)

Preheat oven to 450°F. Heat oil in heavy large skillet over medium heat. Add vegetables, garlic, thyme and bay leaf and cook, stirring frequently, until browned, about 7 minutes. Add goose neck, heart, gizzard and wing tips to skillet and cook, stirring, until browned, about 5 minutes. Remove from heat and stir in parsley.

Pat goose dry with paper towels. Sprinkle cavity with salt and pepper. Spoon half of vegetable mixture into goose. Truss goose. Transfer to deep roasting pan. Roast until browned on all sides, turning every 5 minutes, about 20 minutes total. Reduce oven to 325°F.

Add flour to vegetables remaining in skillet. Place over medium-low heat and stir until browned, about 5 minutes. Whisk in chicken stock and wine, increase heat to medium high and bring to simmer, stirring. Add to goose, cover goose and continue roasting until drumsticks move slightly in sockets and juices from fleshiest part of drumstick run clear when flesh is pricked, about 1¾ to 2 hours, turning goose over halfway into cooking time.

Transfer goose to heated platter. Discard stuffing from cavity. Strain braising liquid into bowl and degrease. Pour into sauceboat. Garnish goose as desired. Pass sauce separately.

4 ❦ Game Birds

What exactly is a game bird? In the past, it was a wildfowl, a creature of the woods or field that a lucky hunter was sometimes able to bag and bring home for the table. Today, however, the term is applied to a number of birds, some of them wild and some not. We present a quartet in this chapter—pheasant, quail, squab and Cornish hens. They are very different birds, but they share a hint of the outdoors in their flavor—which is why, as far as the cook is concerned, all four are considered game birds.

Pheasant and quail are still, usually, caught in the wild. Each has a distinctive tangy, almost smoky taste that can be mild or strong depending on the bird's age. The tiny, plump quail are particularly good when grilled or barbecued, and the recipe for Smoked Herb-seasoned Quail (page 89)—an Alabama specialty—is an excellent way to show them off. Pheasant is prepared a number of ways: When boned, it is the basis of a rich and elegant terrine (page 84); whole, as in Pheasant Souvaroff (page 84), it can be made into a sophisticated game "pie" flavored with brandy, wild mushrooms and truffles.

Squab—the French *pigeonneau*—has been domesticated in this country for years, and is milder in flavor than its wild cousins. The recipes here feature squab roasted and served with a honey sauce (page 85); boned, braised and presented in a mold of winter vegetables (page 86); and, for a very different taste, minced and then stir-fried with rice noodles and Chinese mushrooms (page 88).

Cornish game hen is an American invention, achieved by crossing the Plymouth Rock hen with the Cornish gamecock. It resembles chicken in texture and flavor, but its ancestry gives it an intriguing touch of "gaminess." Many cooks find the size of these birds appealing: A small one will serve one person handily, while a larger one will suffice for two. Game hens adapt well to any number of treatments, and here we find them flavored with everything from spinach and sage (page 91) to apricots (page 91) to Cognac (page 92).

One more trait these birds have in common: Whether they are from the field or from the farm, they all provide an easy way to offer dinner guests something a bit unexpected.

 Pheasant

Pheasant Souvaroff

*From Le Petit Pier in
Tahoe Vista, California.*

2 servings

2 tablespoons clarified butter (see
  footnote, page 11)
1 2- to 2½-pound pheasant
2 tablespoons Cognac
½ cup white wine
3 ounces pheasant Demi-glace (see
  recipe, page 109)
¼ cup Madeira
2 ounces small mushrooms, halved
  and sautéed in 1 to 2 tablespoons
  clarified butter

2 ounces sliced cèpes *or* canned
  wild mushrooms
2 morels, halved
2 to 3 slices pâté de foie gras
1 truffle, sliced
  Salt and freshly ground pepper
1 sheet puff pastry
1 egg, well beaten

Melt butter in large skillet over medium-high heat. Add pheasant and brown on
all sides, about 15 minutes. Warm Cognac in small saucepan over medium heat.
Pour over pheasant and ignite, shaking pan gently. Let burn briefly, then pour
white wine over. Stir in demi-glace, Madeira, sautéed mushrooms, cèpes and
morels. Reduce heat to low, cover and braise 20 minutes.

    Preheat oven to 375°F. Transfer pheasant to baking dish. Arrange foie gras
over top. Stir sliced truffle into sauce. Season sauce with salt and pepper. Pour
sauce over pheasant. Cover dish with puff pastry, carefully sealing to edges. Brush
pastry with beaten egg. Bake until pastry is crisp and golden brown, about 30
minutes. Serve immediately at table: Break through puff pastry, transfer pheasant
to serving platter and carve. Accompany each serving with pastry and sauce.

Terrine de Faisan le St. Germain

*Pheasant Terrine is best
served the day it is made.*

8 servings

1 2½-pound pheasant
¼ cup Madeira
¼ cup Cognac

2¼ cups water
1 small onion, quartered
1 small carrot, quartered
½ celery stalk
1 parsley sprig

1 pound fresh pork fat, thinly sliced
1 pound pork sausage
½ pound chicken livers
1 shallot, chopped
1 egg

1 ounce chopped truffle (optional)
1½ teaspoons salt
1 teaspoon freshly ground white
  pepper
3 bay leaves
  Pinch of ground thyme

Aspic
2 cups beef consommé
2 teaspoons unflavored gelatin

  Lettuce leaves (garnish)
  Watercress and cherry tomatoes
  (garnishes)

Remove skin and bones from pheasant; reserve. Cut meat into large pieces. Transfer to large bowl. Add Madeira and Cognac. Cover and let marinate for 24 hours
in refrigerator, stirring occasionally.

    Crack pheasant bones. Cut skin into large pieces. Combine bones and skin
in heavy large saucepan. Cook over medium heat, stirring occasionally, until bones
are browned, about 10 to 15 minutes. Add water, onion, carrot, celery and parsley

and bring to simmer. Reduce heat to low, cover and cook 1 hour. Strain mixture, pressing with back of spoon to extract all stock. Return stock to saucepan and cook uncovered over medium-low heat until reduced to ½ cup. Let cool, then refrigerate until using.

Preheat oven to 450°F. Line bottom and sides of 8½ × 5 × 4-inch loaf pan with about ⅔ of pork-fat slices and set aside. Drain pheasant meat, reserving marinade. Transfer meat to large bowl. Add sausage, livers and shallot. Put through coarse blade of meat grinder. Return to bowl; add reserved marinade, egg, truffle, salt and pepper. Warm reduced pheasant stock over low heat just until melted. Add to meat mixture and blend well. Turn into prepared pan, smoothing surface. Cover with slices of pork fat. Top with bay leaves and sprinkle with thyme. Place terrine in larger pan. Add enough boiling water to come halfway up sides of terrine. Bake 15 minutes. Reduce oven temperature to 375°F and continue baking until juices run clear and meat thermometer inserted in center of terrine registers 185°F, about 1¾ to 2 hours. Remove from water bath. Place 2-pound weight atop terrine and cool completely. Remove weight and chill terrine about 2 hours.

For aspic: Pour consommé into small saucepan and sprinkle with gelatin. Let stand 5 minutes or until gelatin is softened. Place over low heat and stir until gelatin is dissolved. Cool to room temperature. Discard any accumulated fat from surface of terrine. Carefully pour aspic over terrine. Refrigerate until aspic is firm.

To serve, line platter with lettuce. Unmold terrine onto platter aspic side up. Garnish with watercress and cherry tomatoes.

🍒 Squab and Quail

Roast Squab with Honey Sauce
(Pigeonneau Rôti au Miel)

From La Cheminée in King's Beach, California.

2 servings

2 15-ounce squabs
Salt and freshly ground pepper

2 tablespoons oil
2 teaspoons butter

1 teaspoon chopped shallot
¼ cup Port
¼ cup red wine

2 teaspoons honey vinegar *or* apple cider vinegar
1½ cups veal stock
½ teaspoon cornstarch mixed with 1 to 2 tablespoons Port (optional)

1 teaspoon raw honey
Cognac to taste

Discard giblets from squab. Cut off wings and reserve. Tie legs to breast with string. Sprinkle squab and wings with salt and pepper and set aside.

Preheat oven to 450°F. Heat oil and butter in large ovenproof skillet over medium-high heat until very hot. Add squab and wings and cook until crisp and deep brown, turning frequently. Arrange squab in skillet breast side up. Transfer to oven and roast about 15 minutes (for medium rare). Transfer squab and wings to heated platter. Reduce oven temperature to 350°F.

Discard ¾ of fat from skillet. Return skillet to medium heat, add shallot and sauté about 5 seconds *(be careful not to burn)*. Add Port, red wine, vinegar and squab wings and cook until liquid is reduced by half. Add veal stock and continue cooking until liquid is reduced to ⅔ cup (if sauce is too thin, blend in cornstarch mixture and cook to desired consistency).

Slice squab, adding to sauce any juices that have accumulated on platter. Arrange slices in center of platter with wings on either side. Return squab to oven for 2 minutes to heat through.

Meanwhile, stir honey and Cognac into sauce. Season with salt and pepper. Place over medium heat and cook until hot *(do not boil)*. Pour sauce over squab and serve immediately.

Braised Boned Squab in Mold of Vegetables
(Pigeonneau en Chartreuse)

4 servings

6 tablespoons clarified unsalted butter (see footnote, page 11)
4 squabs
   Salt and freshly ground pepper

4 slices bacon, diced
2 onions, chopped
1 2-pound cabbage, cored, quartered and coarsely chopped

2 cups veal stock mixed with 1 tablespoon cornstarch

Pinch of sugar

Vegetable Mold
¼ cup (or more) clarified unsalted butter (see footnote for recipe, page 11)

4 large carrots (at least 1 inch in diameter), peeled
6 large turnips, peeled
1 small bunch broccoli

Meat glaze (optional)

Heat 6 tablespoons butter in large shallow ovenproof skillet over medium-high heat. Season squab with salt and pepper and brown sides and backs in butter *(breasts will brown later in oven)*. Remove squab; discard butter.

Preheat oven to 450°F. Add bacon, then onions, to same pan and sauté until onion is translucent. Reduce heat, add cabbage and cook slowly uncovered, stirring occasionally, 20 minutes.

Blend in stock. Set squab, breast side up, on cabbage and bake uncovered 10 minutes. Remove from oven and let squab cool until easy to handle.

Meanwhile, drain liquid from cabbage mixture through sieve into large saucepan *(cabbage must be very well drained or mold will not hold its shape)*; set aside for sauce. Season cabbage with sugar and salt and pepper.

To bone squab: Using sharp boning knife, cut squab at joints to remove legs and thighs. Cut along sides of breastbone and remove whole breasts including wings from each. Separate wings from breasts and remove meat. (Save wing bones to make stock.) Chop carcasses and add to pan with liquid from cabbage.

For molds: Butter four 8-ounce soufflé dishes (4 inches in diameter) using at least 1 tablespoon butter in each.

Cook carrots, turnips and broccoli in boiling salted water until just crisp-tender. Drain and let cool briefly. Using largest turnip, cut 4 slices ⅛ inch thick and about 3½ inches wide. Cut 1-inch rosette from center of each and discard. Set slices in bottom of each mold.

Cut carrots into 1½-inch lengths, then cut lengthwise into slices ⅛ inch thick. (You will need about 20 slices.) Slice turnips and cut into 20 pieces same size as carrot. Alternating carrot and turnip, overlap slices vertically around sides of molds. Set broccoli floret side down in center cutout. Cover with layer of drained cabbage, then boned squab, then remaining cabbage. Press with fingers to firm ingredients. *(Molds can be made up to 1 day ahead to this point.)*

When ready to cook, preheat oven to 300°F. Cover top of each mold with parchment paper circles. Set in shallow pan and add hot water to come 1 inch up sides of molds. Bake just until heated through, 10 to 15 minutes.

For sauce: Simmer stock mixture until thickened and reduced. Taste and add meat glaze if needed to highlight flavor and color. Strain through sieve.

To serve, turn mold on its side and press with spoon to remove any excess liquid. Turn each onto dinner plate and surround with small amount of sauce.

Boned Squab with Garlic Sauce
(Pigeonneaux à Sauce l'Ail)

6 servings

6 14-ounce squabs, dressed (reserve livers)
Salt and freshly ground pepper

7 tablespoons unsalted butter
36 garlic cloves, unpeeled

½ cup dry white wine (preferably Chablis)

½ cup chicken stock (preferably homemade)
3 tablespoons brandy

24 medium mushrooms, trimmed
Chicken Quenelles (see following recipe)

Have butcher bone squabs without cutting them open (this is called glove boning), or do it yourself (reserve all bones for making stock).* Season squabs lightly with salt and pepper.

Preheat oven to 450°F. Melt 4 tablespoons butter in large ovenproof skillet over medium-high heat. Add squabs and sauté until browned on all sides. Add garlic and brown quickly. Transfer to oven and roast, basting occasionally, until squabs are done, 20 to 25 minutes.

Transfer squabs and garlic to serving platter and keep warm. Deglaze skillet with wine. Peel 12 cloves of garlic and crush with flat of knife. Add to skillet.

Melt 1 tablespoon butter in small skillet over medium-high heat. Add reserved livers and sauté until evenly browned but still pink inside. Transfer to processor or blender and puree to paste. Add a bit of wine mixture and blend well. Stir livers back into remaining wine mixture. Add stock and brandy, place pan over low heat and simmer until sauce is heated through.

Meanwhile, melt remaining 2 tablespoons butter in large skillet over medium heat. Add mushrooms and sauté until golden. Pour sauce over squabs and garnish platter with mushrooms, remaining garlic cloves and Chicken Quenelles. Serve.

*To bone squab, use sharp boning knife and scissors. Flash freeze squab until some ice crystals have formed. Clean out cavity. Rinse bird under cool water and pat dry with paper towels. Trim wings at joint, discarding tips. Stand bird upright. Using sharp knife, cut through wings where they join body. Loosen meat from breastbones by inserting fingers between meat and carcass along keel bone and pushing against bone toward bottom. (You may want to scrape with knife from time to time instead of just using fingers.) Do not be concerned if small bits of meat come away from skin, since any small pieces can be returned to cavity after boning. Turn bird over onto breast and carefully loosen meat from back by pushing with fingers or scraping with knife. Gradually turn skin inside out as you work. Cut thigh bones from joints using scissors and discard carcass. Turn bird skin side out, feeling for any small bones you may have missed; discard.

Chicken Quenelles

Makes about 6 dozen small quenelles

1 pound boned and skinned chicken breast
1 teaspoon salt
½ teaspoon freshly ground pepper
¼ teaspoon freshly grated nutmeg

2 egg whites, lightly beaten
2 cups whipping cream

Hot salted water *or* chicken stock (for poaching)

Grind chicken finely in processor or with meat grinder. Add salt, pepper and nutmeg and blend well. Gradually add egg whites, mixing vigorously after each addition. Gradually add cream and mix until mixture is firm enough to hold shape. (If mixing by hand, when adding cream, set bowl into larger bowl filled with cracked ice. Beat in cream by tablespoons.)

Generously butter large skillet. Dip 2 teaspoons into boiling water. Heap some of chicken mixture on 1 spoon and round it off with second spoon. Dip second spoon into hot water again, slip it under oval and slide quenelle into buttered skillet. Repeat until quenelles line skillet in single layer *(do not crowd)*. Slowly add enough hot salted water or stock to skillet to float quenelles. Bring liquid to simmer over low heat and poach quenelles until firm, about 5 to 10 minutes *(do not boil)*. Remove with slotted spoon and drain well on paper towels.

Minced Squab

4 to 6 servings

Oil (for deep frying)
¼ pound rice stick noodles (mai fun)*
1 head iceberg lettuce, trimmed and cut in half
¼ cup peanut oil
2 small squabs, boned and finely chopped *or* 1 7- to 8-ounce chicken thigh, skinned, boned and finely chopped
2 green onions (white part only), minced
1 dozen rehydrated dried oriental black mushrooms, minced

1 cup water chestnuts, minced
2 to 3 tablespoons minced prosciutto *or* other cooked ham
Small piece fresh ginger, peeled and crushed
1 tablespoon Sherry
1 tablespoon oyster sauce*
1 tablespoon soy sauce
1 tablespoon cornstarch dissolved in 2 tablespoons water
½ teaspoon sesame oil*
½ teaspoon sugar
Pinch of freshly ground white pepper

Heat oil in deep fryer to about 375°F, until a test noodle puffs without turning brown. *(If noodle turns brown, the oil is too hot.)* While oil is heating, pull noodles apart to separate. Add a few at a time and fry until puffed, about 1 to 2 seconds. Remove with slotted spoon and drain on paper towels. Crush rice sticks slightly and arrange on platter.

Remove outer leaves from lettuce one by one and set on separate platter.

Heat peanut oil in wok or large skillet. Add squab and green onions and stir-fry briefly. Add next 4 ingredients and continue stir-frying 2 to 3 minutes. Add remaining ingredients and stir-fry 1 minute. Spoon over fried noodles and serve.

*Available in oriental markets.

English Roast Chicken with Herbed Orange Stuffing

Roast Turkey and
French Stuffing with Sausage

Irwin Horowitz

Roast Goose with Apple-Sage Dressing

Chinese Duck with Plum Sauce and Pancakes

Hunan-Style Crispy Duck

Smoked Herb-seasoned Quail

Hickory chips give this dish an extra-special flavor.

12 servings

24 quail
⅓ cup vinegar
3 tablespoons chopped fresh sage leaves *or* 1 tablespoon dried sage
1 tablespoon chopped fresh oregano *or* 1 teaspoon dried oregano
1 tablespoon Worcestershire sauce
2 large garlic cloves, minced
1 teaspoon chopped fresh thyme *or* generous ¼ teaspoon dried thyme

1 teaspoon chopped fresh rosemary *or* generous ¼ teaspoon dried rosemary
1 teaspoon sugar
¼ teaspoon freshly grated nutmeg
1½ cups vegetable oil

Salt and freshly ground pepper
24 thin bacon slices

Pat quail dry. Arrange in single layer in large nonaluminum container. Mix vinegar, sage, oregano, Worcestershire sauce, garlic, thyme, rosemary, sugar and nutmeg in large bowl. Whisk in oil 1 drop at a time. Pour marinade over quail. Cover tightly and refrigerate several hours or overnight, turning quail in marinade often.

Prepare barbecue grill, heating coals until white. Meanwhile, combine 2 cups hickory chips with enough water to cover; let stand until coals are ready. Drain quail; pat dry. Season with salt and pepper to taste. Wrap each quail in bacon strip; secure bacon in place with wooden pick if necessary.

Drain hickory chips. Sprinkle chips over hot coals. Cover grill and heat coals until smoke appears around rim. Arrange quail on grill rack. Cover and smoke until leg bones move easily, about 10 minutes, turning occasionally. Transfer to platter and serve.

🌱 *Cornish Game Hens*

Roasted Cornish Game Hens with Citrus Sauce

8 servings

Candied Citrus Peel
1 medium Valencia orange
1 medium grapefruit
1 cup water
½ cup sugar
⅛ teaspoon fresh lemon juice

8 1-pound Cornish game hens* (preferably fresh), wing tips cut off and reserved for stock with necks, gizzards and hearts

Stock
4 cups water
3 celery tops
1 leek top
¼ large carrot

¼ medium onion
½ bay leaf
3 peppercorns
1 fresh thyme sprig *or* pinch of dried
Several parsley stems

Marinade
2 cups dry red wine
2 medium Valencia oranges
2 medium grapefruits
2 teaspoons firmly packed brown sugar
Salt and freshly ground pepper

8 tablespoons (1 stick) butter

Sauce
- 2 tablespoons (¼ stick) butter
- ¼ cup minced shallot
- 3 tablespoons Beurre Manié**

- ¼ cup orange liqueur
- Salt and freshly ground pepper
- 2 tablespoons (¼ stick) unsalted butter

For candied peel: Remove peel *(colored part only)* of orange and grapefruit with vegetable peeler; reserve fruit for marinade. Cut into very fine, long julienne. Transfer to small saucepan. Cover with cold water and bring to boil. Drain and repeat. Drain well. Combine 1 cup water with ½ cup sugar and lemon juice in small saucepan. Place over low heat and cook, swirling pan gently, until sugar is dissolved. Increase heat slightly and bring syrup to simmer. Reduce heat, add fruit peel julienne and simmer very gently until peel is softened and sugar is absorbed, about 30 minutes; *do not boil.* Turn out onto waxed paper, separating strands with knife tip. Cool completely. *(Candied citrus peel can be prepared several months ahead and refrigerated in airtight container.)*

For stock: Combine reserved wing tips, necks, gizzards and hearts with remaining stock ingredients in 6-quart saucepan and bring to boil over medium-high heat. Reduce heat, cover partially and simmer, skimming frequently, until liquid is reduced to 2 cups. Strain into bowl, pressing on vegetables with back of spoon to extract all liquid. Let cool. Degrease surface of stock. Set aside. *(Stock can be prepared several days ahead and refrigerated or frozen.)*

For marinade: Pour wine into large nonaluminum bowl. Holding fruit over wine, remove peel from 2 oranges and 2 grapefruits using vegetable peeler. Squeeze enough orange and grapefruit juice to measure 2 cups, using reserved fruit if necessary. Strain and add juice to wine mixture. Stir in brown sugar, blending well. Season with salt and pepper. Add game hens. Cover and refrigerate overnight, turning occasionally.

Preheat oven to 400°F. Pat birds dry (reserve marinade) and truss. Season with salt and pepper. Rub 1 tablespoon butter over each bird. Arrange birds breast side down on rack in large roasting pan. Roast, turning breast side up, then breast side down every 10 to 15 minutes, until tender and browned and juices run clear when pricked with fork, about 40 to 45 minutes. Meanwhile, pour reserved marinade into large saucepan. Place over high heat and reduce to 2 cups; set aside for sauce. Pour any juices that have accumulated in cavities of birds into roasting pan. Transfer birds to heated serving platter breast side down. Cover, set aside and keep warm.

For sauce: Degrease pan juices and set pan aside. Melt 2 tablespoons butter in large skillet over low heat. Add shallot and cook until soft. Blend in reduced marinade, reserved stock and pan juices. Increase heat to medium high and cook until reduced to about 2 cups. Whisk in 1½ tablespoons Beurre Manié, blending well. Add remaining Beurre Manié if necessary to thicken sauce. Stir in liqueur. Season with salt and pepper. Whisk in unsalted butter 1 tablespoon at a time.

To serve, glaze top of each bird with sauce. Garnish tops with small mound of candied citrus peel. Serve immediately. Pass remaining sauce separately.

*Four 2-pound hens can be substituted. Rub each bird with 2 tablespoons butter and roast at 400°F for about 1 hour. To serve, cut birds in half down center.

**For Beurre Manié, whisk together 1½ tablespoons butter (room temperature) with 1½ tablespoons all purpose flour.

Apricot Game Hens

6 servings

1 cup Chunky Apricot Preserves
(see following recipe)
⅓ cup dry white wine
¼ cup (½ stick) butter, melted
2 8-ounce packages stuffing mix
¾ cup pecans

6 Cornish game hens, thawed,
rinsed and patted dry
Salt and freshly ground pepper
Parsley *or* watercress sprigs
(garnish)

Preheat oven to 350°F. Combine first 3 ingredients in small bowl. Prepare stuffing mix according to package directions and stir in pecans. Sprinkle hens inside and out with salt and pepper. Fill loosely with stuffing, spooning remainder into small baking dish. Truss hens securely. Arrange in roasting pan. Brush each hen generously with some of apricot sauce. Bake hens and remaining stuffing, basting hens frequently until done, about 1 hour. Spoon remaining stuffing onto serving platter and arrange hens on top. Garnish with parsley or watercress.

Chunky Apricot Preserves

This easy preserve also makes delightful gifts.

Makes about 3½ cups

1 6-ounce package dried apricots
1 cup water
4 cups sugar
1 8¼-ounce can crushed pineapple
packed in its own juice,
undrained

1 10-ounce package frozen yellow
squash, thawed and drained
(optional)

Combine apricots and water in medium saucepan and let stand about 1 hour to plump. Place over medium heat and cook until apricots are tender, about 10 minutes. Mash into coarse chunks. Add sugar, pineapple and squash, blending well. Continue cooking over low heat until thickened, stirring occasionally, about 15 minutes. Pour into sterilized jars and seal. Let cool. Store in refrigerator.

Game Hens with Spinach-Sage Stuffing

6 servings

3 bunches fresh spinach (about 2½
pounds), stems removed

¼ cup finely chopped leek
4 tarragon sprigs *or* 4 teaspoons
dried
1 small garlic clove
1 cup (2 sticks) butte
Salt and freshly ground white
pepper

6 Cornish game hens
3 lemons, quartered (remove peel in
fine julienne slices)
12 fresh sage leaves
½ cup dry vermouth
Salt and freshly ground white
pepper

Wash spinach thoroughly. Shake to remove excess water. Transfer to 5- to 6-quart saucepan or Dutch oven and cook over low heat until wilted, stirring occasionally, about 4 to 5 minutes. Drain thoroughly.

Combine leek, tarragon and garlic in processor or blender in batches and puree. Add butter and spinach and puree again. Season with salt and white pepper.

Preheat oven to 450°F. Stuff each hen with 2 lemon quarters and 2 sage leaves. Starting at neck cavity, carefully separate skin from breast using fingers, being careful not to tear skin. Spoon spinach mixture between skin and meat, pressing gently to distribute evenly. Arrange game hens, breast side up, in shallow large pan. Pour in vermouth. Sprinkle lemon julienne over top. Sprinkle with salt and white pepper to taste. Roast 10 minutes. Baste hens with pan juices. Reduce oven temperature to 350°F. Continue roasting, basting frequently, until skin is crisp, juices run clear when bird is pricked with fork and meat thermometer inserted in thickest part of meat without touching bone registers 180°F, about 20 to 30 minutes. Arrange hens on serving platter; spoon pan juices over birds.

Glazed Game Hens with Master Sauce

The master sauce can be refrigerated or frozen and used to simmer other meats.

4 to 6 servings

Master Sauce
 8 cups water
 1 cup heavy soy sauce
 ½ cup light soy sauce
 ½ cup dry Sherry
 3 tablespoons sugar
 1 whole dried red chili
 1 large piece fresh tangerine peel
 5 ½-inch-thick slices fresh ginger, unpeeled
 2 teaspoons whole cloves
 ½ teaspoon freshly ground Szechwan pepper*

 2 cinnamon sticks
 2 whole star anise*

 2 large fresh game hens, trussed, room temperature

Variation
 2 cups peanut oil *or* corn oil for deep frying
 Plum sauce*
 Hot Chinese mustard*

For sauce: Combine first 12 ingredients in heavy 4-quart saucepan or Dutch oven and mix well. Place pan over low heat and simmer 1 hour.

Add game hens to sauce breast side down. Return liquid to low boil. Reduce heat to low and simmer game hens 10 minutes. Turn off heat. Cover pot and let game hens steep in liquid 1 hour. Drain hens well, reserving liquid if desired. Cool hens completely. Cut into serving pieces, quartering breasts. Serve game hens at room temperature or refrigerate and serve cold.

For variation: After simmering game hens 10 minutes, remove from sauce and dry thoroughly with paper towels. Transfer hens to wire rack and let dry at room temperature at least 4 hours.

Heat oil for deep frying in wok or deep saucepan to 375°F. Add game hens one at a time and fry, ladling oil over top until golden, about 5 minutes. Drain well on paper towels and dry thoroughly. Chop into bite-size pieces. Serve immediately or at room temperature. Accompany with plum sauce or Chinese mustard.

*Available in oriental markets.

Game Hens in Cognac Sauce

4 servings

 2 Cornish game hens, split in half
 Salt and freshly ground pepper
 ¼ cup (½ stick) butter
 1 tablespoon oil
 ½ pound mushrooms, sliced

 2 small rosemary sprigs *or* ½ teaspoon dried rosemary
 Cooked wild rice *or* herb rice
 2 tablespoons Cognac
 ½ cup whipping cream

Season hens with salt and pepper. Melt butter with oil in heavy large skillet over medium-high heat until hot but not smoking. Add hens and brown well on all sides. Add mushrooms and rosemary. Reduce heat to low, cover and cook until hens are tender, about 20 minutes. Spread freshly cooked rice on heated platter. Warm Cognac in small saucepan over low heat. Sprinkle Cognac over hens and ignite, shaking pan gently until flame subsides. Set hens over rice. Add cream to skillet and cook gently about 5 minutes, whisking often. Spoon sauce over hens and rice and serve.

Grape-stuffed Cornish Game Hens with Orange Butter

2 servings

2 **Cornish game hens**
2 **tablespoons (¼ stick) butter, room temperature**
1 **tablespoon finely grated orange peel**
1 **teaspoon minced fresh ginger**
1 **teaspoon minced shallot**

Stuffing
2 **tablespoons (¼ stick) butter**
½ **onion, chopped (about ¾ cup)**

2 **slices day-old white bread (crusts trimmed), cubed**
2 **tablespoons minced fresh parsley**
½ **teaspoon dried thyme**
½ **cup seedless red grapes *or* black grapes**
Salt and freshly ground pepper

2 **tablespoons (¼ stick) butter, melted**
1 **tablespoon soy sauce**

Make pocket in breast of each hen by carefully loosening skin with fingers. Combine 2 tablespoons butter with orange peel, ginger and shallot in small bowl and mix until smooth. Place half of butter mixture in each pocket and spread evenly by gently pressing down on skin with fingertips.

For stuffing: Melt 2 tablespoons butter in saucepan over low heat. Add onion and sauté until golden, about 7 minutes. Add bread, parsley and thyme and mix well. Blend in grapes. Taste and season with salt and pepper. Stuff hens with mixture and truss securely.

Position rack in lower third of oven and preheat to 425°F. Combine melted butter and soy sauce in small bowl. Brush over hens. Arrange hens on sides on rack in roasting pan. Roast 10 minutes. Turn hens to other side and roast 10 minutes. Reduce oven temperature to 375°F. Turn hens breast side up and continue roasting until juices run clear when pricked with a fork, about 40 minutes.

Smoked Cornish Game Hens

Here's an excellent recipe for the barbecue enthusiast. You'll need 2 to 4 cups of hickory chips and about 10 pounds of charcoal briquets. Smoked hens can be frozen up to 1 month. Serve at room temperature.

12 servings

2 garlic cloves, lightly crushed
2 lemons, cut in half
6 1½-pound Cornish game hens

¼ cup salt
¼ cup dried rosemary
1 tablespoon freshly ground pepper

To prepare smoker,* soak 2 to 4 cups hickory chips in water 30 to 45 minutes. Meanwhile, arrange charcoal in bottom of smoker. Ignite and allow to burn until gray ash forms, about 45 to 60 minutes.

Rub garlic and lemon in cavity of each hen. Combine salt, rosemary and pepper in small bowl. Rub about ⅓ into cavities. Rub another ⅓ beneath skin, lifting skin as much as possible but taking care to avoid tearing. Sprinkle exterior of hens with remaining seasoning. Truss birds.**

When charcoal is ready, drain hickory chips. Sprinkle about 1 cup over briquets. Arrange hens breast side up in smoker and cook according to manufacturer's directions, adding hickory chips as needed. After 45 minutes turn hens breast side down and cook 30 minutes. Turn hens breast side up and continue cooking until juices in cavities run clear and meat thermometer registers 185°F, about 15 to 30 minutes. Serve hot, at room temperature or chilled.

*If smoker is unavailable, a covered gas grill can be used. Arrange charcoal in bottom of barbecue on one side only and preheat 5 minutes. Arrange hens on opposite side of grill. Cover and cook as directed in recipe.
**To truss hens: Use single thin string to avoid marking the skin. Insert needle through back and tie. Draw legs together and forward, make a figure eight and tie, pulling legs together snugly. Do not draw string across breast of hen.

5 ❦ Stuffings and Sauces

An interesting sauce or a flavorful stuffing—or both—can transform a poultry dish from the merely great to the superb. This is certainly not news. Cooks have been stuffing and saucing poultry for as long as there have been kitchens, if not longer. But there are always new answers to the question of what to put into or on top of a bird, and in creative hands the possibilities are almost infinite.

Turkey wouldn't be turkey without stuffing, of course, but it is by no means the only type of poultry that benefits from such accoutrements. With that in mind, many of the stuffings in this chapter are also designed to go well with goose, duck, chicken and Cornish hens. The recipes range from the traditional and down-home, such as an American Victorian version (page 96), to more exotic ones like Feta and Walnut Stuffing (page 106) or Mexican Picadillo Stuffing (page 104). They are based on everything from corn bread and rice to kasha, sauerkraut, bulgur and chestnuts, and are inspired by national favorites from Greece, India, China and Armenia as well as France and Italy and places closer to home.

A collection of good sauces for poultry is as important to the cook as an assortment of good pots and pans. And one of the wonderful things about poultry is that it marries well with almost any sauce imaginable. The sauces here reflect that adaptability: There are piquant ones, such as Green Peppercorn Sauce (page 109); a zesty Javanese Curry Sauce (page 107); fresh tasting combinations like Cucumber-Dill Sauce (page 108); a hint of sweetness here and there as in Amaretto-Apricot Sauce (page 109); and a trio of barbecue sauces that will bring any party to life.

Many more intriguing sauces and stuffings can be found with individual recipes throughout the book. Their number may not actually reach infinity, but they will certainly take your poultry cooking to a higher plane.

🍎 *Stuffings*

American Victorian Turkey Stuffing

A very moist traditional stuffing.

Makes about 16 cups

1 1-pound loaf unsliced white bread, cut into ½-inch cubes
½ pound unsliced egg bread, cut into ½-inch cubes
2 to 3 slices rye bread (crusts trimmed), torn into small pieces (¾ cup)

½ cup (1 stick) butter
3 medium onions, finely chopped
½ large bunch celery (including leaves), chopped
3 ounces mushrooms, sliced (about 5 medium)

6 ounces canned chestnuts (about 1 cup), rinsed, drained and chopped *or* 15 fresh chestnuts, blanched, peeled and chopped

½ pound fresh sausage
1 turkey liver, chopped
½ teaspoon dried sage
½ teaspoon dried thyme
Salt and freshly ground pepper
3½ to 4 cups chicken stock
2 eggs, well beaten

1 pint oysters (with liquor)

Preheat oven to 275°F. Combine white, egg and rye breads in large roasting pan. Bake until crisp and dry, stirring frequently, about 30 minutes.

Meanwhile, melt butter in large skillet over medium heat. Add onions and celery; cover and cook, stirring occasionally, until onion is lightly golden, about 10 to 15 minutes. Add mushrooms; cover and cook, stirring occasionally, 10 minutes. Stir onion mixture into bread with chestnuts.

Cook sausage in medium skillet over medium-high heat until browned, breaking up meat with fork. Discard all but 1 tablespoon fat. Stir sausage into bread mixture. Add turkey liver to same skillet and cook over medium heat until outside is browned, stirring frequently. Add to bread mixture with seasoning. Blend in stock and eggs.

Poach oysters in liquor in small saucepan over medium heat until just translucent, about 4 minutes. Drain oysters; cut in half. Blend into stuffing. Cool briefly; refrigerate before using.

French Stuffing with Sausage

Makes about 6 cups

1 tablespoon butter
1 medium onion, chopped
2 medium shallots, minced
½ pound fresh, mildly seasoned sausage
1½ cups soft breadcrumbs
½ cup hot chicken stock
2 pounds fresh chestnuts, blanched, peeled and coarsely chopped *or* 3 cups canned chestnuts, rinsed, drained and coarsely chopped

6 medium mushrooms, chopped
2 medium celery stalks, trimmed and chopped
¼ cup brandy
2 tablespoons Madeira
1 tablespoon minced fresh parsley
1 teaspoon dried thyme
⅛ teaspoon allspice
Salt and freshly ground pepper

Melt butter in large skillet over medium heat. Add onion and shallots and cook until soft, stirring occasionally, about 8 minutes. Add sausage, increase heat to medium high and cook, breaking up meat with fork, until browned. Discard excess fat. Moisten breadcrumbs with stock and add to sausage mixture with all remaining ingredients, blending well. Place over medium heat and cook, stirring occasionally, about 5 minutes. Cool briefly; refrigerate before using.

Louisiana Corn Bread Stuffing

Makes about 5 cups

¼ cup (½ stick) butter
¼ cup finely chopped green onion
¼ cup finely chopped green bell pepper
¼ cup finely chopped celery
3 cups coarse Herbed Buttermilk Corn Bread crumbs (see following recipe)
3 cups stale French breadcrumbs

¼ cup finely chopped fresh parsley
Salt and freshly ground pepper
Ground red pepper
1½ cups chicken stock (preferably homemade)
2 eggs
1 tablespoon butter, cut into small pieces

Preheat oven to 350°F. Grease 2-quart baking dish. Melt ¼ cup butter in heavy large skillet over low heat. Add onion, green pepper and celery and cook, stirring frequently, until limp but not browned, about 10 minutes. Stir in crumbs, parsley, salt and pepper and red pepper. Blend chicken stock and eggs in small bowl. Add to corn bread mixture and stir until evenly moistened. Turn into prepared baking dish. Dot with 1 tablespoon butter. Bake until browned, 35 minutes.

Herbed Buttermilk Corn Bread

Makes one 8- or 9-inch square pan of corn bread

1 cup yellow cornmeal
½ cup all purpose flour
1 teaspoon salt
1 teaspoon baking powder
½ teaspoon baking soda

½ teaspoon dried thyme
1 cup buttermilk
1 egg, beaten
2 tablespoons (¼ stick) butter, melted

Preheat oven to 400°F. Grease 8- or 9-inch square pan and place in oven. Sift dry ingredients into medium bowl. Stir in buttermilk, egg and melted butter. Turn batter into heated pan. Bake until bread is puffed and browned and tester inserted in center comes out clean, about 20 minutes.

Herman's Corn Bread Stuffing

Stuffing can be prepared up to 3 days ahead. Cover and store in refrigerator, or freeze up to 1 month. Thaw completely in refrigerator before using. Leftover cooked stuffing can be frozen.

Makes enough stuffing for a 12- to 15-pound turkey

½ cup dry white wine
¼ cup chopped dried apricots
¼ cup raisins

½ cup (1 stick) butter
5 shallots, chopped
1 large onion, chopped
¼ pound chicken livers, chopped
½ cup pine nuts, toasted
¼ cup slivered almonds, toasted
1 garlic clove, minced

Herbed Corn Bread (see following recipe), crumbled

1 cup steamed rice
1 1-pound can whole chestnuts, drained
¼ cup honey
1 tart apple, cored and chopped
1 teaspoon ground ginger
1 teaspoon dried basil
½ teaspoon allspice
½ teaspoon dried thyme
½ teaspoon dried oregano
Salt and freshly ground pepper

Combine wine, apricots and raisins. Set aside.

Melt butter in large skillet over medium-high heat. Add shallots and onion and cook until soft. Add chicken livers, nuts and garlic and continue cooking, stirring constantly, until livers are just firm. Stir in wine-fruit mixture and cook over high heat 2 minutes.

Turn into large mixing bowl and blend in remaining ingredients.

Herbed Corn Bread

An easy-to-prepare moist bread that is excellent with any meat or poultry dish.

Can be frozen up to 3 months.

Makes one 8-inch square pan of corn bread

1 cup yellow cornmeal	¼ teaspoon dried savory
1 cup unbleached all purpose flour	⅛ teaspoon dried thyme
2 tablespoons sugar	Pinch of celery seed
1 tablespoon plus ½ teaspoon baking powder	1 cup milk
1 teaspoon salt	¼ cup (½ stick) butter, melted and cooled
4 green onions, minced	1 egg
¼ teaspoon fresh sage, crumbled	

Preheat oven to 425°F. Grease 8-inch square metal baking pan.

Sift cornmeal, flour, sugar, baking powder and salt into mixing bowl. Add onion and herbs and blend well.

In another bowl, beat milk, butter and egg until foamy. Add dry ingredients and stir just to combine *(mixture should be lumpy; do not overblend)*.

Turn into prepared pan and bake until corn bread tests done, about 30 minutes. Remove from oven and let cool 10 minutes in pan. Invert onto rack and cool to room temperature. (If not using for stuffing, cut into squares and serve.)

Saffron Rice Stuffing with Sausage

This is one of the infinite variations of paella, Spain's national dish.

Makes about 4 cups

2 tablespoons olive oil	1 turkey liver *or* 2 chicken livers, chopped
1 small onion, minced	1 medium tomato, peeled, seeded and coarsely chopped
1 large garlic clove, minced	½ cup shelled peas (½ pound unshelled)
1 medium-size green bell pepper, roasted, peeled, seeded and minced	⅓ cup pitted black olives *or* green olives, thinly sliced
1 medium-size red bell pepper, roasted, peeled, seeded and minced *or* 2 ounces pimientos, rinsed and minced	2 cups chicken stock
1 cup uncooked rice	¾ teaspoon saffron threads, crushed
1 ounce diced good-quality smoked ham (preferably Black Forest *or* Bayonne type)	¼ teaspoon paprika
1 diced cooked garlic sausage (such as linguisa *or* kielbasa)*	Salt and freshly ground pepper

Heat oil in heavy large skillet over low heat. Add onion, garlic and peppers. Cover and cook 15 minutes, stirring occasionally. Add rice, ham, sausage and liver and stir until well coated with oil. Add tomato, peas, olives and stock and bring to boil. Stir in saffron and paprika. Reduce heat, cover and simmer until liquid is absorbed, 20 to 30 minutes. Add salt and pepper.

*To substitute sausage that is purchased uncooked, dice, sauté until browned and drain well.

Oriental Rice Stuffing with Sausage and Cabbage

This is also a delicious side dish for a home-cooked Chinese dinner.

Makes about 4 cups

1½ cups uncooked glutinous rice*

6 dried oriental mushrooms*

2 tablespoons Shaohsing rice wine** *or* dry Sherry
1 tablespoon soy sauce
1 tablespoon oyster sauce**
1 tablespoon yellow bean sauce**

3 tablespoons peanut oil
⅓ cup unsalted cashews *or* peanuts (preferably raw)
1 tablespoon minced fresh ginger

1 tablespoon minced green onion
1 cup diced Bok choy (Chinese cabbage)
1 Chinese sausage,** thinly sliced
1 turkey liver *or* 2 chicken livers, chopped
Salt *or* soy sauce (optional)

Wash rice thoroughly and discard any foreign particles. Cover with cold water and soak at least 4 hours. Drain well.

Arrange on thin layer of cheesecloth in steamer. Set over hot water and steam until rice is cooked, about 45 minutes. *(Can be prepared ahead and reheated.)*

Meanwhile, soak mushrooms in enough tepid water to cover for 30 minutes. Drain well; squeeze out excess moisture. Cut mushrooms into julienne slices, discarding hard central core.

Mix wine and soy, oyster and bean sauces in small bowl and set aside.

Heat oil in wok. Add cashews and stir-fry until browned. Remove from wok. Add ginger and onion and cook 1 minute. Add cabbage, sausage, liver and mushrooms and stir-fry until cabbage is tender. Add wine mixture, cashews and rice and mix well. Season with salt or additional soy sauce if necessary.

*Glutinous rice, also called sweet or starchy rice, is available in oriental markets.
**Available in oriental markets.

Rice Stuffing with Salsa Verde and Pumpkin Seeds

Celebrate any occasion with a Latin American stuffing chock-full of tomatillos, chilies and pumpkin seeds.

Makes about 4 cups

1 pound fresh tomatillos, husked *or* 1 15- or 16-ounce can, drained
3 fresh large poblano chilies (⅓ pound), roasted, peeled and seeded *or* 4 canned whole chilies
⅓ cup pumpkin seeds, toasted
1 large garlic clove
¼ teaspoon ground cumin
Pinch of sugar (optional)
1 cup (about) chicken stock

2 tablespoons olive oil
⅓ cup minced green onion (white part only)

1 to 2 jalapeño chilies, seeded and minced
1¼ cups uncooked rice
Salt and freshly ground pepper
1 tablespoon minced fresh cilantro (coriander) *or* Italian parsley
Sour cream (garnish)
2 avocados, peeled, seeded and sliced (garnish)
Deep-fried plantains *or* sweet potatoes (optional)

Puree first 5 ingredients with pinch of sugar in processor or blender. Strain through fine sieve, pressing vegetables with back of spoon to extract as much liquid as possible. Add enough chicken stock to equal 2½ cups.

Heat olive oil in heavy large skillet over low heat. Add green onion and jalapeño chilies. Cover and set aside for 10 minutes, stirring occasionally. Mix in rice, coating evenly with oil. Blend in puree and bring to simmer. Cover and cook until all liquid is absorbed, about 40 minutes. Taste and season with salt and pepper. Just before serving, stir in cilantro. Top with sour cream and garnish with avocados. Surround with plantains or sweet potatoes if desired.

Fragrant Indian Rice Stuffing

Makes about 6 cups

2 cups water
1 cup uncooked brown rice

2 tablespoons oil
2 large onions, sliced
1 garlic clove, minced
12 medium mushrooms, sliced (about 2 cups)
½ cup raisins
2 teaspoons minced fresh ginger

¼ teaspoon ground cardamom
¼ teaspoon cinnamon
¼ teaspoon freshly ground pepper
⅛ teaspoon ground cloves
4 ounces unsalted cashews, roasted and coarsely chopped (about ⅔ cup)
1 cup chicken stock

Combine water and rice in medium saucepan and bring to boil over high heat. Reduce heat to low, cover and simmer until rice is tender and water is absorbed, about 40 minutes.

Heat oil in large skillet over medium heat. Add onions and garlic, cover and cook, stirring occasionally, until onion is translucent, about 10 minutes. Add mushrooms, raisins, ginger and spices and cook until mushrooms are soft, about 5 minutes. Remove from heat. Stir in rice and cashews. Add stock. Cool briefly; refrigerate before using.

Kasha Stuffing with Mushrooms, Leeks and Wild Rice

Wild rice adds texture to the kasha, but you may omit it for a more authentic version of the Russian original.

Makes about 7 cups

½ cup uncooked wild rice
1½ cups chicken stock
2 teaspoons salt
2 tablespoons (¼ stick) unsalted butter

2 tablespoons rendered chicken fat *or* unsalted butter
1 large onion, finely chopped
1 large leek (white part only), halved lengthwise and thinly sliced
6 ounces mushrooms, sliced

½ cup walnuts, chopped
1 cup kasha (buckwheat groats) mixed with 1 lightly beaten egg
2 cups chicken stock
2 tablespoons (¼ stick) unsalted butter
½ teaspoon dill seed *or* dried dillweed
Salt and freshly ground pepper
¾ cup sour cream, room temperature

Wash rice thoroughly and discard any foreign particles. Bring stock and salt to boil in heavy medium saucepan. Slowly stir in rice. Reduce heat, cover and simmer until rice is tender and liquid is absorbed, about 45 minutes. Remove from heat and stir in butter. Set aside.

Melt chicken fat in heavy large saucepan over medium-high heat. Add onion and sauté until browned. Reduce heat to low. Add leek, cover and set aside, stirring occasionally, until leek is translucent, about 15 minutes. Increase heat to medium high. Add mushrooms and walnuts and sauté until mushroom liquid is evaporated, about 5 minutes. Increase heat to high, add kasha and stir until grains separate, about 3 minutes. Add stock, butter and dill and bring to boil. Reduce heat, cover and simmer until liquid is absorbed, about 15 minutes. Stir in rice. Season to taste with salt and pepper. Blend in sour cream just before serving.

Armenian Stuffing with Bulgur

A good partner for Cornish game hens or chicken.

Makes about 11 cups

1 cup (2 sticks) butter
2 large onions, chopped
1½ teaspoons ground coriander
½ teaspoon ground cumin
1½ cups slivered blanched almonds
1½ cups dried apricots, coarsely chopped

1½ cups raisins
4 cups cooked bulgur
2 teaspoons cinnamon
½ teaspoon ground cloves
Salt and freshly ground pepper

Melt butter in large skillet over medium heat. Add onions, coriander and cumin; cover and cook, stirring occasionally, until onion is translucent, about 10 minutes. Add almonds, apricot and raisins and cook uncovered, stirring occasionally, until almonds are golden. Transfer to large bowl. Add bulgur, cinnamon, cloves and salt and pepper and toss well. Cool briefly; refrigerate before using.

German Sauerkraut Stuffing

Nice with turkey, goose or duck.

Makes about 7 cups

2 tablespoons (¼ stick) butter
1 large onion, finely chopped
1 medium-size tart apple, peeled, cored and diced
3 pounds sauerkraut, rinsed in warm water and drained well

1 tablespoon caraway seed
12 juniper berries
½ cup dry white wine
Salt and freshly ground pepper

Melt butter in large skillet over medium heat. Add onion and apple and cook until soft, stirring occasionally, about 6 minutes. Blend in sauerkraut, caraway seed and juniper berries. Reduce heat to low and cook, stirring occasionally, 8 to 10 minutes. Add wine, increase heat to medium and cook until all liquid is absorbed. Discard juniper berries. Season stuffing with salt and freshly ground pepper. Cool briefly; refrigerate before using.

South American Stuffing

Makes about 8 cups

2 tablespoons olive oil
2 medium onions, chopped
¾ cup chopped green bell pepper
8 ounces ground pork
2 cups ground almonds, toasted (8 to 9 ounces)
4 slices firm white bread, cut into small cubes

3 hard-cooked eggs, coarsely chopped
1 cup chopped pitted prunes
1 cup pimiento-stuffed green olives, halved (5 ounces)
½ teaspoon dried thyme
Salt and freshly ground pepper

Heat oil in large skillet over medium heat. Add 2 chopped onions with green pepper, cover and cook until onion is translucent but not browned, about 10 minutes, stirring occasionally. Add pork and cook until browned, breaking up meat with fork. Remove from heat; discard any excess fat. Mix in almonds, bread, eggs, prunes, olives and thyme. Season with salt and pepper. Cool briefly, then refrigerate thoroughly before using.

Italian Stuffing with Fruits and Nuts

Makes 7 to 8 cups

4 ounces bacon (preferably nitrite free), chopped
18 fresh chestnuts, blanched, peeled and coarsely chopped *or* 7 ounces canned chestnuts (about 1¼ cups), rinsed, drained and coarsely chopped
8 ounces ground turkey, chicken *or* veal
3 apples, peeled, cored and diced
3 ripe pears, peeled, cored and diced

1⅓ cups chopped pitted prunes (8 ounces)
½ cup freshly grated Parmesan cheese (2 ounces)
6 tablespoons (¾ stick) butter, melted
12 walnut halves, chopped
¼ teaspoon freshly grated nutmeg
Salt and freshly ground pepper

Sauté bacon in heavy large skillet over medium-high heat until cooked through. Drain well on paper towels. Transfer to large bowl. Add remaining ingredients and blend well. Let cool, then refrigerate thoroughly before using.

Mushroom, Prosciutto and Pine Nut Stuffing

A hearty stuffing reminiscent of sunny Italy.

Makes about 4 cups

1¼ ounces dried Italian mushrooms

2 tablespoons (¼ stick) unsalted butter
1 2-inch piece bone marrow, minced
1 small onion, minced
1 large garlic clove, minced
1¼ pounds mushrooms, sliced
⅓ cup dry Marsala
1½ ounces prosciutto *or* cooked ham, diced

¾ cup whipping cream
½ cup fresh breadcrumbs
¼ cup freshly grated Parmesan cheese
3 tablespoons pine nuts, toasted
1 teaspoon fresh lemon juice
1 teaspoon minced fresh thyme *or* ½ teaspoon dried
½ teaspoon minced fresh sage *or* ⅛ teaspoon dried
Salt and freshly ground pepper

Soak dried mushrooms in enough tepid water to cover for at least 30 minutes. Drain well, reserving soaking liquid. Transfer mushrooms to sieve and rinse thoroughly. Chop mushrooms coarsely. Strain soaking liquid through sieve lined with dampened paper towel.

Melt butter and bone marrow in heavy large skillet over low heat. Add onion and garlic. Cover and cook, stirring occasionally, until translucent, about 10 minutes. Increase heat to medium high, add fresh mushrooms and sauté until pieces separate and liquid is evaporated. Add Marsala, dried mushrooms and strained liquid and simmer over medium-high heat until liquid is absorbed. Remove from heat and add remaining ingredients, mixing lightly. Cool briefly; refrigerate before using.

Greek Stuffing with Pine Nuts

Makes about 5½ cups

1½ cups chicken stock
¾ cup uncooked rice

2 tablespoons (¼ stick) butter
4 green onions, minced
1 pound lean ground turkey, chicken *or* veal
⅓ cup pine nuts

½ cup water, at boiling point
3 tablespoons minced fresh parsley
4 juniper berries
1 small bay leaf, crumbled
¼ teaspoon ground sage
Salt and freshly ground pepper
⅔ cup raisins

Bring stock to boil in medium saucepan over high heat. Stir in rice. Reduce heat to low, cover and simmer until rice is cooked. Set aside.

Melt butter in large skillet over medium heat. Add green onions and stir until soft, 2 to 3 minutes. Reduce heat to low. Add ground meat and pine nuts and cook until meat loses pink color, breaking up meat with fork, 3 to 4 minutes. Discard any excess fat. Stir in rice, boiling water, parsley, juniper berries, bay leaf and sage. Increase heat to medium and cook, stirring occasionally, until all liquid is absorbed. Discard juniper berries. Season stuffing with salt and pepper. Stir in raisins. Cool briefly; refrigerate before using.

Pork, Red Cabbage and Chestnut Stuffing

Makes about 4 cups

18 unpeeled whole chestnuts*
½ cup (about) milk
½ cup (about) veal stock *or* chicken stock

3 cups (8 ounces) shredded red cabbage
½ cup dry red wine
2 tablespoons red wine vinegar
2 tablespoons (¼ stick) unsalted butter, cut into pieces
1 tart large apple, peeled, cored and coarsely chopped

8 thick slices slab bacon, trimmed
1 medium onion, minced
1 large garlic clove, minced

1½ pounds ground pork, *or* ¾ pounds ground pork and ¾ pound ground veal
1 turkey liver *or* 2 chicken livers, diced
½ cup fresh breadcrumbs
2 tablespoons red wine vinegar
2 tablespoons raisins plumped in tepid water for 15 minutes (optional)
1½ teaspoons minced fresh thyme *or* ½ teaspoon dried
Salt and freshly ground pepper
2 eggs, lightly beaten

Cut strip off one side of each chestnut shell. Blanch nuts in large saucepan of boiling water 5 minutes. Remove chestnuts from water one at a time and peel off outer shell and inner brown skin. *(Leave difficult-to-peel chestnuts in water a bit longer.)* Pour out water and return chestnuts to pan. Add enough milk and stock to come 1 inch above chestnuts. Simmer gently until chestnuts are just tender when pierced with knife, about 50 minutes. Drain well.

Preheat oven to 400°F. Blanch cabbage in large saucepan of boiling salted water for 4 minutes. Drain well and add wine, vinegar, butter and apple. Bring to simmer over direct heat. Cover and bake until cabbage is tender and liquid is absorbed, about 20 minutes.

Blanch bacon in large saucepan of boiling water 10 minutes. Drain well. Cut into small strips, about 1 × ⅓ inch. Transfer to heavy large skillet and brown over medium heat until crisp. Reduce heat to low and add onion and garlic. Cover and cook 10 minutes, stirring occasionally. Increase heat to medium high, add pork and sauté until browned, breaking up with fork. Add liver and sauté until browned and firm, about 1 minute. Remove from heat. Stir in breadcrumbs, vinegar, raisins, thyme, chestnuts and cabbage. Taste and season with salt and pepper. Let cool completely before stirring in eggs. Refrigerate before using.

*One 15-ounce can cooked whole chestnuts can be substituted for fresh. Rinse lightly and drain well before adding.

Chestnut, Apple, Endive and Leek Stuffing

This fruit, nut and vegetable composition is characteristic of the bountiful harvests of the French countryside.

Makes about 4 cups

¼ cup (½ stick) butter
1 large leek (white part only), halved lengthwise and thinly sliced
6 ounces endive, halved lengthwise and sliced
2 tart medium apples, peeled, cored and coarsely chopped

36 whole chestnuts,* unpeeled

1 cup (about) milk
1 cup (about) chicken stock
¼ cup Calvados *or* Cognac
½ cup (about) whipping cream
1 tablespoon fresh lemon juice
Salt and freshly ground pepper
Freshly grated nutmeg
Pinch of sugar (optional)

🦃 Secrets of Perfect Stuffings

According to M. F. K. Fisher, for many Americans there is only one kind of stuffing—oyster. But for those of a more adventuresome frame of mind, there are equally delicious alternatives from every culture. In France a mildly seasoned sausage and fresh chestnut mixture lightly moistened with brandy and Madeira is a popular choice. Germans are partial to a tart apple and sauerkraut blend that is especially good with goose or duck. There are rich fruit stuffings in Italy, and brown rice and spice versions in India. The choices are almost limitless.

What may have begun as a way to make one bird feed many hungry guests has now become an end in itself: For some, having turkey is simply an excuse for having stuffing. So in case you were thinking that you would let the holiday season pass without it, remember the little boy who, when asked if he wanted seconds, said, "No more of the turkey, thanks. But I'd sure like another helping of that bread he ate."

A few tips will help make all of your holiday stuffings perfect:

- Fill poultry just before roasting. Although many steps in a special dinner can be done ahead, this is not one of them.

- Chill stuffing before putting it into bird; this helps prevent spoiling.

- Do not use uncooked pork.

- Fill cavities loosely. Stuffing should not be packed in, because it needs room to expand during cooking to stay light.

- If you have made more stuffing than the bird can hold, spoon excess into baking dish, cover and bake in the same oven. It will take about 1 hour to cook 4 cups of stuffing.

- If you are in a rush because you forgot to put the bird on in time for dinner, you can put all the stuffing into a baking dish and decrease the total roasting time for the bird by five minutes per pound.

- Remove any extra stuffing from bird as soon as dinner is over; cool it quickly and store in a covered container in the refrigerator.

Melt butter in heavy skillet over low heat. Add leek, endive and apples. Cover and stew gently, stirring occasionally until tender, about 20 minutes.

Cut strip off side of each chestnut shell. Blanch nuts in large saucepan of boiling water 5 minutes. Remove chestnuts from water one at a time and peel off outer shell and inner brown skin. *(Leave difficult-to-peel chestnuts in water a bit longer.)* Pour out water and return chestnuts to pan. Add enough milk, stock and Calvados to come 1 inch above chestnuts. Simmer gently until chestnuts are just tender when pierced with knife, about 50 minutes. Gently stir in leek mixture with cream to moisten. Season with lemon juice, salt and pepper, nutmeg and sugar to taste. Cool, then refrigerate before using.

*Two 15-ounce cans cooked whole chestnuts can be substituted for fresh. Rinse lightly and drain well. Toss with 2 tablespoons Calvados or Cognac. Add to leek with cream to moisten. Heat through.

Mexican Picadillo Stuffing

*The chocolate is not read-
ily discernible, but it
heightens the other flavors.*

Makes about 4 cups

2 tablespoons lard *or* olive oil
1 large onion, minced
2 large garlic cloves, minced
8 seeded jalapeño chilies, minced*
2 pounds ground pork *or* beef
3 medium tomatoes, peeled, seeded and coarsely chopped
⅓ cup pitted green olives *or* black olives, quartered
⅓ cup raisins plumped in tepid water for 15 minutes
⅓ cup slivered almonds, toasted

¼ cup *acitrón*** *or* glacéed fruit (optional), coarsely chopped
1 teaspoon red wine vinegar *or* Sherry wine vinegar
¼ teaspoon cinnamon
¼ teaspoon ground cloves
1 ounce Mexican chocolate *or* unsweetened chocolate, melted
½ cup fresh breadcrumbs
Salt and freshly ground pepper
2 eggs, lightly beaten

Melt lard in heavy large skillet over low heat. Add onion, garlic and chilies. Cover and set aside, stirring occasionally, 10 minutes. Increase heat to medium high, add pork and sauté until browned, breaking up with fork. Reduce heat and stir in tomatoes, olives, raisins, almonds, acitrón or glacéed fruit, vinegar, cinnamon and cloves and simmer, stirring occasionally, 15 minutes. Mix in chocolate. Remove from heat and stir in breadcrumbs. Season with salt and pepper. Remove any excess fat with a bulb baster. Let cool completely before stirring in eggs. Refrigerate before using.

*Any fresh, dried or canned chilies can be substituted. Adjust amount to taste.
**Acitrón, a candied cactus, is available in Latin American markets.

Feta and Walnut Stuffing

*Feta, a fresh sheep's-milk
cheese preserved in brine,
is combined here with walnuts and currants, two staples of Greek and Middle
Eastern cooking. This stuffing can also be used as a
filling for phyllo
pastry sheets.*

Makes about 4 cups

2 tablespoons (¼ stick) unsalted butter
1 medium onion, minced
4 cups walnuts, coarsely chopped
2 tablespoons currants *or* raisins plumped in tepid water for 15 minutes

¼ teaspoon freshly grated nutmeg
¼ teaspoon cinnamon
4 ounces feta cheese, crumbled
2 tablespoons minced Italian parsley *or* 1 tablespoon minced fresh mint

Melt butter in heavy small skillet over low heat. Add onion and cover and cook until translucent, stirring occasionally, about 10 minutes. Add walnuts, currants, nutmeg and cinnamon and cook 5 minutes. Remove from heat. Stir in feta and parsley, blending thoroughly. Cool briefly; refrigerate before using.

🍎 *Sauces*

Dick's Barbecue Sauce

Makes about 2 quarts

2 unpeeled lemons, quartered and
  seeded
2 onions, quartered
2 cups water
1 cup (2 sticks) margarine
1 cup cider vinegar

½ cup sugar
¼ cup prepared mustard
2 tablespoons salt
2 teaspoons freshly ground pepper
1 teaspoon ground red pepper

Combine all ingredients in 3-quart saucepan and bring to boil over medium-high heat. Reduce heat and simmer 20 minutes. Transfer to blender or processor in batches and puree until smooth. Let cool. Pour into jar with tight-fitting lid. Store in refrigerator.

Barbecue Sauce and Marinade

This all-purpose sauce is ideal for enhancing chicken breasts.

Makes about 1½ cups

1 tablespoon butter
½ onion, chopped
½ cup water
½ cup catsup
2 tablespoons firmly packed brown
  sugar

1½ tablespoons Worcestershire sauce
1 tablespoon vinegar
1 teaspoon dry mustard

Melt butter in medium skillet over medium-high heat. Add onion and sauté until tender, about 5 minutes. Blend in remaining ingredients. Cook until heated through, about 10 minutes. Let cool slightly in skillet. Transfer to jar and cover tightly. Store in refrigerator.

White Barbecue Sauce

Use this to baste chicken whether baking, broiling or grilling.

Makes about 1 cup

6 tablespoons mayonnaise
2 tablespoons sugar
1 teaspoon salt

1 teaspoon freshly ground pepper
3 tablespoons fresh lemon juice
3 tablespoons vinegar

Combine first 4 ingredients in small bowl. Gradually whisk in lemon juice and vinegar and blend until smooth.

Javanese Curry Sauce

This pungent mixture makes a good base for curries. May be stored in refrigerator up to 1 week; sauce can also be frozen.

Makes 4 cups

- 1 medium onion, finely chopped
- ½ cup cooked ham, finely chopped
- 2 slices uncooked bacon, finely chopped
- ¼ cup curry powder *or* Garam Masala (see following recipe)
- 1 tablespoon all purpose flour
- 1 apple, unpeeled, coarsely chopped
- ¼ cup preserved mango *or* preserved kumquat
- 1 tablespoon tomato paste
- 1 tablespoon fresh lemon juice
- 1 tablespoon honey
- 1 tablespoon salt
- 2 cups chicken stock

Sauté onion, ham and bacon in large skillet over medium heat until onion is golden. Stir in curry powder and cook 1 minute longer.

Blend in flour, then add apple, preserved fruit, tomato paste, lemon juice, honey and salt. Pour in chicken stock and blend thoroughly. Allow to simmer 25 minutes, stirring occasionally. Cool slightly, then stir to blend well.

Garam Masala

This very pungent mixture will permeate grinding and sifting tools, so it is best to set aside tools exclusively for this purpose. Recipe may be halved or doubled.

Makes about ¾ cup

- 2½ ounces coriander seed
- 1 ounce black cardamom seed, peeled
- 1 ounce whole cumin seed or ½ ounce ground
- ½ ounce whole black peppercorns *or* ¼ ounce ground pepper
- ½ ounce whole cloves
- ½ ounce ground cinnamon

Preheat an 8-inch skillet over medium heat. Add whole seeds and spices (not ground) and cook 4 to 5 minutes, stirring frequently. Place in blender with glass (not plastic) container or in small grinder, or use mortar and pestle, mallet or rolling pin, and reduce to powder. Transfer mixture to strainer set over glass or metal bowl. Regrind any pieces left unground. Add cumin and pepper, if not using whole spices, and cinnamon and mix to blend. Store in tightly covered jar.

Lemon Sauce Edouard Nignon

An excellent sauce for roast duck.

Makes about 1 cup

- 4 small lemons
- ¼ cup sugar
- ¼ cup strained fresh lemon juice, *or* to taste
- 2 cups duck Demi-glace (see following recipe)
- 1 teaspoon arrowroot
- 1 teaspoon water
- 2 tablespoons (¼ stick) unsalted butter

Finely grate peel from lemons; set aside. Remove all membrane and pith from 2 lemons and cut into sections; set aside.

Combine sugar with splash of water in heavy 1-quart saucepan. Cook over medium heat to obtain a tea-colored caramel. Add lemon juice and cook a few minutes longer to smooth mixture. Add lemon peel and demi-glace and simmer until reduced to about 1 cup.

When ready to serve, finish sauce by bringing to boil once again. Dissolve arrowroot in water and stir into sauce. Cook briefly until slightly thickened. Remove from heat and whisk in butter. Strain into sauceboat and add lemon sections.

Demi-glace

The basis of several sauces, this is made from the left-over bones and carcass of either cooked or raw poultry. Save the leftover bones and freeze until ready to make demi-glace. Demi-glace can be frozen (1- or 2-cup quantities are handiest) for up to 6 months.

Makes about 1 cup

1 poultry carcass, cooked *or* raw, coarsely chopped
Miscellaneous bones and giblets (do not include liver)
½ pound veal bones (especially marrow bones)

1 tablespoon all purpose flour
1 large onion, chopped

1 large carrot, chopped

Chicken stock, veal stock *or* water, *or* combination
1 large garlic clove
½ bay leaf
1 teaspoon dried thyme
½ teaspoon freshly ground pepper

Preheat oven to 450°F. Place all bones and giblets in roasting pan and let brown at least 1 hour, turning occasionally until an even dark brown.

Sprinkle with flour, add onion and carrot and brown another 15 minutes.

Transfer to deep pot and cover with stock. Add garlic and remaining seasonings and simmer gently at least 4 hours, skimming foam as it accumulates (particularly at beginning of cooking). When stock is rich and brown, pour through very fine strainer into bowl. Cover and chill overnight.

Remove all fat from surface. Turn stock into heavy saucepan and cook very slowly over direct heat until it becomes a gelatinous demi-glace, about 1 hour.

Cucumber-Dill Sauce

Makes 1½ cups

1 large cucumber, peeled, halved lengthwise, seeded and cut into ¼-inch slices
1 teaspoon salt

2 tablespoons (¼ stick) unsalted butter
1 tablespoon minced shallot

1 cup dry vermouth *or* dry white wine

2 tablespoons white wine vinegar (preferably bottled with dill)
1 cup whipping cream
1 tablespoon minced fresh dill *or* mint, *or* 1 teaspoon dried dillweed

Place cucumber in colander and toss with salt. Let drain 30 minutes. Rinse with cold water and shake dry.

Melt butter in heavy saucepan over medium-low heat. Add shallot and cucumber. Place buttered piece of parchment or waxed paper over top and cover pan with lid. Simmer gently until cucumber is just tender, 5 minutes.

Combine vermouth and vinegar in heavy medium saucepan and boil until reduced by half. Add cream and continue boiling until sauce is reduced and thickened. Reduce heat and stir in dill. Add cucumber and just heat through.

Green Peppercorn Sauce

Makes about 2 cups

¼ cup dry white wine
2 tablespoons Cognac
1 to 2 tablespoons green peppercorns (preferably water packed), rinsed and drained

2 cups duck Demi-glace (see recipe, page 109)
1 cup whipping cream
Pinch of salt (optional)

Combine wine and Cognac in heavy 1½- or 2-quart saucepan and simmer until reduced by half. Add green peppercorns and continue cooking until syrupy. Add demi-glace and let simmer another 10 minutes. Finally, add cream and simmer rapidly, stirring constantly, until mixture coats spoon, about 15 minutes longer. Taste and adjust seasoning. Serve immediately.

Amaretto-Apricot Sauce

Makes about 2 cups

½ cup (1 stick) unsalted butter
⅓ cup (about) thinly sliced shallot
¾ cup fresh orange juice, strained
¼ cup (scant) fresh lemon juice
2 tablespoons prepared mustard (preferably Dijon)

2 cups pitted and halved fresh apricots*
Salt and freshly ground pepper
1 cup amaretto
½ cup slivered almonds, toasted

Melt butter in saucepan. Add shallot, orange juice, lemon juice, mustard, apricots and salt and pepper and cook briefly to soften shallot and combine ingredients. Add amaretto and simmer, stirring occasionally, until sauce coats spoon, about 35 minutes. Stir in almonds just before serving.

*If fresh apricots are not available, use canned apricot halves; rebalance "bite" of the sauce by adding 2 tablespoons Cognac and juice of another lemon.

Sauce Salmis

The classic presentation of salmis consists of thin slices of medium-rare duck breast accompanied by crisply browned legs and topped with this sauce.

Makes about 1 cup

1 tablespoon unsalted butter
¼ cup minced shallot
1½ cups good-quality dry red wine
1 cup duck Demi-glace (see recipe, page 109)

4 tablespoons (½ stick) unsalted butter, cut into small pieces

Melt 1 tablespoon butter in small saucepan over medium heat. Add shallot and sauté until softened. Stir in wine and demi-glace and simmer until reduced to scant 1 cup. Pour through fine strainer into another small saucepan. Whisk in remaining butter a little at a time, making sure each piece is absorbed before adding another. Taste and adjust seasoning if necessary.

Oyster-Mushroom Gravy

The perfect complement to Louisiana Corn Bread Stuffing (see recipe, page 97).

4 to 6 servings

6 tablespoons (¾ stick) butter
8 ounces fresh mushrooms, sliced (3 cups)

¼ cup (½ stick) butter
3 tablespoons all purpose flour
3 tablespoons finely chopped green onion
2 cups chicken stock *or* strained oyster liquor, *or* combination

¼ cup dry white wine
½ teaspoon Worcestershire sauce
2½ to 3 dozen fresh oysters, shelled and patted dry
2 tablespoons chopped fresh parsley
Salt and freshly ground pepper

Melt 6 tablespoons butter in heavy large skillet over medium-high heat. Add mushrooms and cook until browned and liquid has evaporated, stirring occasionally, about 5 minutes. Remove with slotted spoon.

Melt ¼ cup butter in same skillet over low heat. Stir in flour and cook, stirring, until mixture is rich brown color, about 10 minutes. Add onion and stir 3 minutes. Blend in stock and wine and bring to simmer. Let simmer until thickened to saucelike consistency. Stir in Worcestershire sauce. Return mushrooms to skillet. Add oysters and bring to gentle simmer *(liquid should be barely shaking)*. Let simmer until oysters are just opaque. Remove from heat and stir in parsley. Season with salt and pepper. Turn into sauceboat.

Brandied Giblet Gravy for Turkey

The giblets can be prepared early in the morning, the gravy finished up with the pan juices just after the turkey comes out of the oven.

Makes about 4 cups

Giblets from one 18- to 20-pound turkey
1 tablespoon unsalted butter
1 large shallot, minced
3 tablespoons Cognac (or more)

Pan juices from one 18- to 20-pound turkey

½ cup Madeira (or more)
⅓ cup all purpose flour
4 cups Poultry Stock (see following recipe), heated
Salt and freshly ground pepper

Trim and discard all tough cartilage from gizzard. Trim and discard fat from heart. Cut gizzard, heart and liver into ¾-inch dice. Melt butter in small skillet over low heat. Add shallot and cook until soft, about 3 minutes, stirring occasionally. Increase heat to medium, add giblets and cook, stirring constantly, 2 to 3 minutes; giblets should remain soft in center. Add 3 tablespoons Cognac to corner of skillet, let warm, then ignite, shaking skillet gently until flames subside. Continue cooking giblets until liquid is reduced to thin glaze (about 2 tablespoons), 2 to 3 minutes, stirring frequently. Let cool for 15 minutes.

Chop giblets finely. Return to skillet and blend with Cognac reduction.

After removing turkey from oven, pour off all fat from juices in roasting pan; reserve ¼ cup fat. Place roasting pan over high heat. Add ½ cup Madeira and stir, scraping up any browned bits. Cook until reduced to 2 tablespoons. Stir in reserved fat. Reduce heat to low, whisk in flour and cook, whisking constantly, until roux is rich nut brown, about 10 minutes. Remove pan from heat and whisk in hot stock. Place pan over medium-high heat and bring to simmer. Stir gravy until thickened to desired consistency (if gravy becomes too thick, blend in up to ¼ cup more Madeira). Season with salt and pepper.

Strain gravy into large saucepan. Add reserved giblets. Place over low heat and cook 3 to 4 minutes to blend flavors. Taste and adjust seasoning. Add 1 to 2 tablespoons more Cognac if desired. Serve immediately.

Poultry Stock

Stock can be prepared ahead and refrigerated or frozen.

Makes 4 cups

3 cups chicken stock (preferably homemade)
3 cups water
1 turkey neck
2 turkey wing tips
1 small onion, peeled and stuck with 1 clove
1 medium carrot, sliced
2 large parsley sprigs
½ bay leaf
½ teaspoon dried thyme

Combine all ingredients in large saucepan and bring to boil over high heat, skimming foam from surface. Reduce heat, cover partially and simmer 45 minutes, skimming frequently. Strain into another saucepan. Let cool. Discard fat from surface. Refrigerate until ready to use.

🍏 Index

Almond-Mustard Sauce, Papillotes
   of Chicken with, 10
Almond Sauce (Murghi dil Bahasht),
   Chicken in, 24
Amaretto-Apricot Sauce, 110
American Victorian Turkey Stuffing,
   96
Apple Brandy Sauce, Chicken in, 7
Apple-Sage Dressing for Roast
   Goose, 82
Apple-Sausage Stuffing (Turkey), 58
Apricot Game Hens, 91
Armenian Stuffing with Bulgur, 101

Barbecue Sauce
   Dick's, 107
   and Marinade, 107
   White, 107
Basil Stuffing for Chicken Legs, 14
Batter-Dipped Chicken, 43
Beer-b-cued Chicken, 16
Blanc de Volaille (Stuffed Chicken
   Breasts), 21
Bordelaise Sauce, Poulet Sauté à la,
   33
Brandied Giblet Gravy for Turkey,
   111
Brioche Filled with Chicken Liver
   Pâté, 53
Broccoli Mayonnaise for Molded
   Chicken Salad, 49
Broiled Ginger Chicken, 15
Brown Sauce, Tomato-Flavored for
   Chicken Sauté, 29
Butterflied Deviled Chicken, 6

Chestnut, Apple, Endive and Leek
   Stuffing, 104
Chèvre and Mushroom-Stuffed
   Chicken Legs, 22
Chicken
   in Almond Sauce, Silky, 24
   Beer-b-cued, 16
   Burgers (Cooked), 52
   Butterflied, Deviled, 6

and Chili Buns (Cooked), 52
Coq au Riesling, 23
Cutting and Boning, 12–13
Double-Fried with Ginger and
   Sesame Oil, 44
Lemon-Tarragon, Grilled, 19
Mexican Tortilla Sandwich
   (Cooked), 53
Mustard, 6
One-Pot with Dumplings, 25
Paprika, Creamy, 24
with Raspberry Vinegar Sauce, 32
Roast, English with Herbed
   Orange Stuffing, 2
Roast, with Rosemary Butter, 2
Roast, Vertical, 4; Basic, 4;
   Variations, 4–5
Salad. See Salad, Chicken
Sauce. See Sauces
Sauté with Asparagus and
   Carrots, 31
Sauté with Mushrooms, Shallots
   and Herbs, 29
Sauté with Red Wine, 30
Steamed in Lotus Leaf,
   Chinatown Restaurant, 26
Sticky, 21
Stuffings. See Stuffings
Teriyaki, 16
Wings-Raviolini Stew, 26
Wings, Stuffed Deep-Fried, 45
Yogurt, 3
Chicken Breasts
   About, 34–35
   in Apple Brandy Sauce, 7
   with Asparagus and Lemon
      Sabayon, 8
   Batter-Dipped, 43
   with Chinese Mushrooms, 7
   Chinese Shredded and Pork with
      Green Chilies, 40
   Dijon Penne, 42
   Dijonnais, Grilled, 16
   Ginger, Short and Sweet, 35
   with Green Peppers, 41

Italian Grilled on Skewers, 18
Jarlsberg, 39
Japanese Yakitori, 18
Kiev, Oven-Baked, 11
Kung Pao, 41
Lemon, Cold, 28
Mediterranean, 40
in Mustard Sauce, Triple, 37
in Oyster Sauce, 39
Papillotes with Almond-Mustard
   Sauce, 10
with Peanut Dipping Sauce, 15
with Pearl Onions and Gratin of
   Mixed Greens, 9
Poached, About, 20
Poached in Butter, 20; in Water-
   Based Liquid, 20
Poached Cold in Walnut Sauce
   (Circassian), 19
Quenelles, 88
Rolls, Vegetable-Filled, 44
Salad. See Salad, Chicken
Sauté with Oranges and
   Avocados, 31
Sesame-Crisped, 3
Singapore Saté, 17
Southern Fried, 43
Steamed (Pepper), with Roasted
   Onion Sauce, 27
Stir-Fried. See Stir-Fried Chicken
for Stuffed Palacsinta (Hungarian
   Pancakes), 36
Stuffed with Vegetable Sauce, 21
Suprêmes de Volaille, About,
   34–35
Szechwan Spicy Tangerine, 42
on Vegetables, Bed of Garden
   (Microwave), 65
-Wrapped Sausages with
   Mushroom-Tomato Sauce, 38
Chicken Legs and Thighs
   Basil Stuffing (Legs) and Tomato-
      Zucchini Sauce, 14
   Boning Legs, 13
   Broiled Ginger, 15

Chèvre and Mushroom-Stuffed (Legs), 22
Italian Grilled on Skewers (Thighs), 18
Oven-Fried Buttermilk (Thighs), 6
in Piquant Liver Sauce (Thighs), 32
Poulet Sauté à la Bordelaise, 33
Singapore Saté, 17
Southern Fried, 43
Tangier Tajine, 25
with Walnuts in Plum Sauce (Thighs), 46
Chicken Liver
-Mushroom Sauté, 54
Pâté, 54; Brioche Filled with, 53
Sauce, Piquant, 32
with Ginger and Sherry, 54
Chili Sauce with Tamarind, 46
Chinese. See also Stir-Fried, Szechwan
Chicken Breasts with Mushrooms, 7
Chicken, Shredded and Pork with Green Chilies, 40
Chicken, Steamed in Lotus Leaf, 26
Chicken with Walnuts in Plum Sauce, 46
Chicken Wings, Stuffed Deep-Fried, 45
Duck, Hunan-Style Crispy, 78
Duck with Plum Sauce, 69
Oriental Chicken (Vertically Roasted), 4
Oriental Rice Stuffing with Sausage and Cabbage, 99
Circassian Chicken (Cold, Poached in Walnut Sauce), 19
Citrus Sauce for Roasted Cornish Game Hens, 90
Cognac and Port (for Vertically Roasted Chicken), 5
Coq au Riesling, 23
Corn Bread, Herbed, 98; Buttermilk, 97
Corn Bread Stuffing, 97
Cornish Game Hens
Apricot, 91
in Cognac Sauce, 92
Glazed with Master Sauce, 92
Grape-Stuffed with Orange Butter, 93
Roasted with Citrus Sauce, 89
Smoked, 94
Stuffing. See Stuffings
Cranberry and Lemon Sauce, Duck with, 70
Cucumber-Dill Sauce, 109
Curried Turkey Salad in Brioche, 66
Curry, Javanese Beer, 65
Curry, Royal Duck, 76
Curry Sauce, Javanese, 108

Daikon Dipping Sauce for Duck, 75
Demiglace, 109

Dijon Penne Chicken, 42
Dijonnais, Grilled Chicken, 16
Deep-Fried, Stuffed Chicken Wings, 45
Double-Fried Chicken with Ginger and Sesame Oil, 44
Dressing. See Mayonnaise, Sauces, Stuffings
Duck
About, 72–73
with Apples and Cider, 79
Breasts with Calvados, 79
Chinese, with Plum Sauce, 69
with Cranberry and Lemon Sauce, 70
Curry, Royal, 76
with Grapes, 70
Hunan-Style, Crispy, 78
Pan-Broiled with Daikon Dipping Sauce, 75
Roast Country, 68
Roast with Fruit-and-Nut Stuffing, 77
Roast in Spicy Sauce, 68
Salad, 80
Sauce. See Sauces
Smoked, Honey-Brined, 74
Stuffing. See Stuffings
Szechwan, 78

Feta and Walnut Stuffing, 106
French Stuffing with Chestnuts and Sausage, 96
Fried Chicken, 6, 43–45
Fruit-and-Nut-Stuffed Roast Duck, 77

Game Birds. See Name of Individual Bird, e.g., Pheasant, Squab, etc.
Game Hens. See Cornish Game Hens
Garam Masala, 108
Garlic and Basil Puree (for Vertically Roasted Chicken), 4
German Sauerkraut Stuffing, 101
Giblet Gravy. See Gravy
Ginger Chicken Breasts, Short and Sweet, 35
Ginger Chicken, Broiled, 15
Glazed Game Hens with Master Sauce, 92
Goose
Braised with Red Wine Sauce, 82
Liver and Pear Salad, 80
Roast, 81; Apple-Sage Dressing, 82
Stuffing, German Sauerkraut, 101
Grape-Stuffed Cornish Game Hens with Orange Butter, 93
Gravy. See also Sauces
Giblet, Brandied, for Turkey, 111
Giblet with Wine, 57
Oyster-Mushroom, 111
Greek Stuffing with Pine Nuts, 103
Green Chili Mayonnaise, 48

Green Peppercorn Sauce, 110
Grilled Chicken, 16–19

Honey-Brined Smoked Duck, 74
Hunan-Style Crispy Duck, 78

Indian Rice Stuffing, Fragrant, 100
Italian Stuffing with Fruits and Nuts, 102
Italian Stuffing, Mushroom, Prosciutto and Pine Nuts, 103

Japanese, 44
Double-Fried Chicken with Ginger and Sesame Oil, 44
Pan-Broiled Duck with Daikon Dipping Sauce, 75
Teriyaki Chicken, 16
Yakitori Chicken, 18
Javanese Beer Curry (Turkey), 65
Javanese Curry Sauce, 108
John's Dressing (Sausage, Mushroom, Apple), 59

Kasha Stuffing with Mushrooms, Leeks and Wild Rice, 100
Kiev Chicken, Oven-Baked, 11
Kung Pao Chicken, 41

Lemon
Chicken, Cold, 28
-Mustard Dressing for Smoked Chicken Salad, 49
Sabayon and Asparagus, Chicken with, 8
Sauce, Edouard Nignon, 108
-Tarragon Chicken, 19
Lime and Green Chili (for Vertically Roasted Chicken), 5
Liver. See Chicken Liver, Goose Liver
Louisiana Corn Bread Stuffing, 97

Mayonnaise. See also Sauces
Basic, 60
Broccoli, 49
Green Chili, 47
Mediterranean Chicken Breasts, 40
Mexican Picadillo Stuffing, 106
Mexican Tortilla Sandwich, 53
Microwave
Turkey Breast on Bed of Garden Vegetables, 65
Turkey Roast, Boned, 65
Turkey, Traditional, 65
Mushroom
and Chèvre Stuffed Legs, 22
-Chicken Liver Sauté, 54
Chinese, Chicken Breasts with, 7
Prosciutto, and Pine Nut Stuffing, 103
-Tomato Sauce, Chicken-Wrapped Sausages with, 38

Mustard. *See also* Sauces
  -Almond Sauce, 10
  Chicken, 6
  Sauce, Triple, 37
  Tarragon, 37
  Three Green Herbs (Trois Herbes Vertes), 38

Oriental Rice Stuffing with Sausage and Cabbage, 99
Oriental Chicken (Vertically Roasted), 4
Oven-Baked Chicken Kiev, 11
Oven-Fried Buttermilk Chicken, 6
Oyster-Mushroom Gravy, 111
Oyster Sauce, Chicken in, 39
Oyster Sesame Sauce for Steamed Chicken, 27

Palacsinta (Hungarian Pancake), Chicken-Stuffed, with Paprika and Sour Cream, 36
Pan-Broiled Duck with Daikon Dipping Sauce, 75
Papillotes of Chicken with Almond-Mustard Sauce, 10
Paprika Chicken, Creamy, 24
Pasta Chicken Salad with Fruit, 48
Pâté, Chicken Liver, 54
Peanut Dipping Sauce, Chicken with, 15
Pepper-Steamed Chicken with Roasted Onion Sauce, 27
Pheasant Souvaroff, 84
Pheasant, Terrine de Faisan le St. Germain, 84
Plum Sauce, Chicken with Walnuts in, 46
Poached. *See* Chicken Breasts, Poached
Pork, Red Cabbage and Chestnut Stuffing, 104
Port and Chestnut Sauce, Roast Duck with, 71
Poulet Sauté à la Bordelaise, 33
Poultry Stock, 112

Quail, Smoked Herb-Seasoned, 89
Quenelles, Chicken, 88

Raspberry Vinegar Sauce, Chicken with, 32
Rice Stuffing
  Brown and Mushroom (for Turkey Thigh), 59
  Fragrant Indian, 100
  Saffron with Sausage, 98
  with Salsa Verde and Pumpkin Seeds, 99
Rice, Wild, Chicken Salad with, 50
Roast. *See* Poultry to be Roasted, e.g., Chicken, Duck, etc.

Saffron Rice Stuffing with Sausage, 98
Salad, Chicken
  and Melon with Green Chili Mayonnaise, 47
  Molded, 49
  and Pasta with Fruit, 48
  Sesame, 48
  Smoked, Apple and Walnut, 49
  Stir-Fried with Szechwan Noodles, 51
  Walnut, 47
  with Wild Rice, 50
Salad, Duck, 80
Salad, Turkey
  with Almonds and Ginger, 66
  Curried in Brioche, 66
  Tonnato, 60
Sandwiches
  Chicken Burgers, 52
  Chicken and Chili Buns, 52
  Mexican Tortillas, 53
Saté, Singapore, 17
Sauce(s). *See also* Gravy, Mayonnaise, Mustard
  Almond-Mustard for Chicken Papillotes, 10
  Almond, Silky, Chicken in, 24
  Amaretto-Apricot, 110
  Apple Brandy, Chicken in, 7
  Apricot Preserves for Game Hens, 91
  Barbecue, 107
  Bordelaise, Poulet Sauté à la, 33
  Brown, Tomato-Flavored, Chicken Sauté with, 29
  Chili with Tamarind for Stuffed Chicken Wings, 46
  Citrus for Game Hens, 90
  Cognac for Game Hens, 92
  Cranberry and Lemon for Duck, 70
  Cucumber-Dill, 109
  Curry, Javanese, 108
  Curry, Javanese Beer, 65
  Daikon Dipping for Broiled Duck, 75
  Demi-Glace, 109
  Garlic for Boned Squab, 87
  Green Peppercorn, 110
  Honey for Roast Squab, 85
  Jarlsberg for Chicken, 39
  Lemon, Edouard Nignon, for Duck, 108
  Lemon-Mustard Dressing for Smoked Chicken Salad, 49
  Lemon Sabayon for Chicken and Asparagus, 8
  Master for Cornish Game Hens, 92
  Mediterranean, for Chicken Breasts, 40
  Mushroom-Tomato for Chicken-Wrapped Sausages, 38

Mustard, Triple, Chicken in, 37
Onion, Roasted for Pepper-Steamed Chicken, 27
Oyster, Chicken in, 39
Oyster Sesame for Steamed Chicken, 27
Paprika and Sour Cream, Hungarian, 36
Peanut Dipping, Chicken with, 15
Piquant Liver, Chicken in, 32
Plum for Chicken with Walnuts, 46
Port and Chestnut for Duck, 71
Raspberry Vinegar, Chicken with, 32
Salmis, for Duck, 110
Spicy for Roast Duck, 68
Teriyaki for Chicken, 16
Tomato Dipping for Vegetable-Filled Breast Rolls, 44
Tomato-Zucchini for Chicken Legs, 14
Tonnato for Turkey Salad, 61
Vegetable for Stuffed Chicken Breasts, 21
Vinaigrette Dressing for Duck Salad, 80
Vinegar, Duck with, 74
Walnut for Cold Poached Chicken, 19
Sauté. *See* Chicken Sauté, Chicken Liver
Sesame Chicken Salad, 48
Sesame-Crisped Chicken, 3
Smoked Chicken, Apple and Walnut Salad, 49
Smoked Cornish Game Hens, 94
Smoked Herb-Seasoned Quail, 89
South American Stuffing, 102
Southern Fried Chicken, 43
Spices, Sweet (for Vertically Roasted Chicken), 5
Squab
  Boned with Garlic Sauce, 87
  Braised, Boned in Mold of Vegetables, 86
  Minced, 88
  Roast with Honey Sauce, 85
Steamed. *See* Chicken, Chicken Breasts
Stew, Chicken-Raviolini, 26
Sticky Chicken, 21
Stir-Fried. *See also* Chinese, Szechwan
Stir-Fried Chicken
  Chinese Shredded and Pork with Green Chilies, 40
  Dijon Penne, 42
  Double-Fried with Ginger and Sesame Oil, 44
  with Green Peppers, 41
  Kung Pao, 41
  Lemon, Cold, 28
  Salad with Szechwan Noodles, 51

Stir-Fried Chicken (*continued*)
Szechwan Spicy Tangerine, 42
with Walnuts in Plum Sauce, 46
Stir-Fried Duck, Royal Curry, 76
Stir-Fried Squab, Minced, 88
Stock, Poultry, 112
Stuffed. *See* Poultry to be Stuffed,
e.g., Chicken Breasts, Turkey
Thighs
Stuffings
About, 105; Chicken Breasts, 35
American Victorian Turkey, 96
Apple-Sage Dressing for Roast
Goose, 82
Apple-Sausage (Turkey), 58
Armenian with Bulgur, 101
Basil for Chicken Legs, 14
Chestnut, Apple, Endive and
Leek, 104
Chèvre and Mushroom for
Chicken Legs, 22
Corn Bread for Turkey, 97
Feta and Walnut, 106
French (Chestnut and Sausage),
96
Fruit-and-Nut for Duck, 77
Grape for Cornish Game Hens,
93
Greek with Pine Nuts, 103
Herbed Orange for Roast
Chicken, 2
Italian with Fruits and Nuts, 102
John's Dressing (Sausage,
Mushroom and Apple), 59
Kasha with Mushrooms, Leeks
and Wild Rice, 100
Mexican Picadillo, 106

Mushroom, Prosciutto and Pine
Nuts, 103
Pork, Red Cabbage and Chestnut,
104
Rice, Brown and Mushrooms for
Turkey, 59
Rice, Fragrant Indian, 100
Rice, Oriental with Sausage and
Cabbage, 99
Rice, Saffron with Sausage, 98
Rice with Salsa Verde and
Pumpkin Seeds, 99
Sauerkraut, German, 101
South American, 102
Spinach-Sage for Game Hens, 91
Venetian with Cheese for Turkey,
56
Suprêmes de Volaille, About, 34–35
Szechwan Duck, 78
Szechwan Noodles, Stir-Fried
Chicken Salad with, 51
Szechwan, Spicy Tangerine Chicken,
42

Tangier Tajine (Chicken Legs and
Thighs), 25
Tarragon Mustard, 37
Teriyaki Chicken, 16
Terrine de Faisan le St. Germain
(Pheasant), 84
Tomato-Zucchini Sauce for Stuffed
Chicken Legs, 14
Tonnato Sauce (for Turkey Salad),
61
Turkey
Braised with Lemon and
Cinnamon, 63
Breast on Bed of Garden
Vegetables (Microwave), 65
Breast, à l'Orange, 58
Breast, Paupiettes with Creamed
Chestnuts, 61

Breast, Valdostana, 62
Curry, Javanese Beer (Cooked),
65
Elegant (Cooked), 63
Gravy, Giblet Brandied, 111
Gravy, Giblet with Wine, 57
Mole (Thigh), 64
Roast, with Apple-Sausage
Stuffing, 57
Roast, Boned (Microwave), 65
Roast, Upside-Down, 56
Salad with Almonds and Ginger,
66
Salad, Curried in Brioche, 66
Stuffing. *See* Stuffings
Thigh, Stuffed, 59
Tonnato (Salad), 60
Traditional, in Microwave, 65

Vegetable-Filled Chicken Breast
Rolls, 44
Vegetable Sauce for Stuffed Chicken
Breasts, 21
Venetian Stuffing with Cheese for
Turkey, 56
Vinaigrette Dressing for Duck Salad,
80
Vinegar Sauce, Duck with, 74

Walnut-Chicken Salad, 47
Walnut Sauce for Cold Poached
Chicken, 19
Wild Rice, Chicken Salad with, 50

Yogurt Chicken, 3

🍎 Credits and Acknowledgments

The following people contributed the recipes included in this book:

Ahmed's/Henri IV, Cambridge, Massachusetts
Mary Jo Giambellucca Anderson
Rebecca Anasis
Nancy Baggett
Nancy Barocci
Joan and Wade Baxley
James Beard
Susan Beegel
Terry Bell
Jennifer Brennan
Marian Burros
Anne Byrd
Sharon Cadwallader
Cafe Roma, San Luis Obispo, California, Maria Rosa Rizzo and Steve True, chefs
Hugh Carpenter
La Cheminée, King's Beach, California, Jean-Pierre Doignon and Tommy Cortopassi, chef-owners
Christiania Inn, Heavenly Valley, California, Austin Angell, chef
Mary Beth Clark
Curds and Whey, Oakland, California
Mary Danio
Kay Domurot
Leslie Dougan
Ernie's, San Francisco, California, Victor and Roland Gotti, owners; Jacky Robert, chef
Chuck Flannery-Jones
Phyllis Fox-Krupp
Le Francais, Wheeling, Illinois, Jean Banchet, chef-owner
Robert and Shelley Friedman and Ken and Phyllis Nobel
Grace Ann Gaskill
Peggy Glass
Connie Glenn
Phyllis Gorenstein
Marion Gorman
Freddi Greenberg
Connie Grigsby
Barbara Harris
Hilarie's, Santa Cruz, California
Jim Holmes
Bill Hughes
Roger Jaloux
Ellie Johnson
Jane Helsel Joseph
Madeleine Kamman
Barbara Karoff
Lynne Kasper

Sharon Katz
Saralee Kucera
Alma Lach
Aiko Lee
Rita Leinwand
Faye Levy
Scott and Darlene Lieblich
Amy Lovett
Nan and Ivan Lyons
The Mandarin, San Francisco, California, Cecilia Chiang, owner
Abby Mandel
Joel McCormick
Barbara McGrath
Perla Meyers
Ming Gate, Hampton, Virginia
Nancy Mock
Jinx and Jefferson Morgan
Lori Openden
Helen Cassidy Page
The Paradise Cafe, Chicago, Illinois
Les Pastoureaux, Paris, France
Le Petit Pier, Lake Tahoe, Nevada, Jean Dufau, chef-owner
Thelma Pressman
Le Rhône, San Francisco, California, Georges Chalaye, chef-owner
Julie Sahni
Le St. Germain, Los Angeles, California
Richard Sax
Sharon Sheehy
Edena Sheldon
Spago, Los Angeles, California, Wolfgang Puck, chef-owner
Karyn Taylor
Megan Timothy
Doris Tobias
May Wong Trent
Jan Weimer
Alice Welsh
Anne Willan
Gahan Wilson and Nancy Winters
Janet and Roger Yaseen

Additional text was supplied by:

Marian Burros, *Secrets of Perfect Stuffings*
Lynne Kasper, *The Vertically Roasted Chicken*
Rita Leinwand, *Suprêmes de Volaille*
Thelma Pressman, *Traditional Turkey in Your Microwave*
Jan Weimer, *Poaching Chicken Breasts, Cutting and Boning Chicken*
Janet and Roger Yaseen, *Tips for a Perfect Duck*

Photographs styled by:

Edena Sheldon, cover, Grape-Stuffed Cornish Game Hens, Chinese Duck with Plum Sauce, and salads spread

Accessories information

for cover: Sabattini Silver accessories, imported from Italy and courtesy of Richard Ginori, 9555 Santa Monica Blvd., Beverly Hills, California 90210. Glazed tiles courtesy of International Tile & Supply Corp., 1288 South La Brea Avenue, Los Angeles, California 90019. *Grape-Stuffed Cornish Game Hens:* Armetale platter and goblets, "Obernai" patterned dinnerware imported from France, "Calibri" flatware, all linens courtesy of The Brass Tree, 9044 Burton Way, Beverly Hills, California 90211. *salads spread:* Zani stainless steel accessories, imported from Italy and Este ceramic dinner plate, imported from Italy, courtesy of Richard Ginori. *Chinese Duck with Plum Sauce:* Antique Chinese picnic basket, "Celadon," imported dinner plates and platter courtesy of The Brass Tree. Hand-painted Oriental silk paneled screen, hand-painted silk fan, oval brass and reed tray, solid brass service plates, brass and reed bowl courtesy of Geary's, 351 North Beverly Drive, Beverly Hills, California 90210.

Special thanks to:

Marilou Vaughan, *Editor, Bon Appétit*
Bernard Rotondo, *Art Director, Bon Appétit*
William J. Garry, *Managing Editor, Bon Appétit*
Barbara Varnum, *Articles Editor, Bon Appétit*
Jane Matyas, *Associate Food Editor, Bon Appétit*
Brenda Koplin, *Copy Editor, Bon Appétit*
Judith Strausberg, *Copy Editor, Bon Appétit*
Robin G. Richardson, *Research Coordinator, Bon Appétit*
Leslie A. Dame, *Assistant Editor, Bon Appétit*
Donna Clipperton, *Manager, Rights and Permissions, Knapp Communications Corporation*
Karen Legier, *Rights and Permissions Coordinator, Knapp Communications Corporation*
Rose Grant
Elaine Linden
Mary Nadler
Sylvia Tidwell

The Knapp Press
is a wholly owned subsidiary of
KNAPP COMMUNICATIONS CORPORATION.
Chairman and Chief Executive Officer:
Cleon T. Knapp
President: H. Stephen Cranston
Senior Vice-Presidents:
  Rosalie Bruno *(New Venture
    Development)*
  Betsy Wood Knapp *(MIS Electronic
    Media)*
  Harry Myers *(Magazine Group
    Publisher)*
  William J. N. Porter *(Corporate
    Product Sales)*
  Paige Rense *(Editorial)*
  L. James Wade, Jr. *(Finance)*

THE KNAPP PRESS

President: Alice Bandy; *Administrative Assistant:* Beth Bell; *Editor:* Norman Kolpas; *Managing Editor:* Pamela Mosher; *Associate Editor/Cookbooks:* Diane Rossen Worthington; *Associate Editors:* Jeff Book, Jan Koot, Sarah Lifton; *Assistant Editors:* Colleen Dunn Bates, Nancy D. Roberts; *Art Director:* Paula Schlosser; *Designer:* Robin Murawski; *Book Production Manager:* Larry Cooke; *Book Production Coordinators:* Veronica Losorelli, Joan Valentine; *Director, Rosebud Books:* Robert Groag; *Financial Manager:* Joseph Goodman; *Assistant Finance Manager:* Kerri Culbertson; *Financial Assistant:* Julie Mason; *Fulfillment Services Manager:* Virginia Parry; *Director of Public Relations:* Jan B. Fox; *Marketing Assistants:* Dolores Briqueleur, Randy Levin; *Promotions Managers:* Joanne Denison, Nina Gerwin; *Special Sales Manager:* Lynn Blocker; *Special Sales Coordinator:* Amy Hershman

This book is set in Sabon, a face designed by Jan Teischold in 1967 and based on early fonts engraved by Garamond and Granjon.

Composition was on the Mergenthaler Linotron 202 by Graphic Typesetting Service.

Series design by Paula Schlosser.

Text stock: Knapp Cookbook Opaque, basis 65. Color plate stock: Mead Northcote basis 70. Both furnished by WWF Paper Corporation West.

Color separations by NEC Incorporated.

Printing and binding by R. R. Donnelley and Sons.